Gilda O'Neill (1951-2010) took three university degrees and was awarded an honorary doctorate for her work on the East End. In 1990 O'Neill began writing full-time. She published thirteen novels and six works of non-fiction, including *East End Tales*. She also broadcasted, gave talks and wrote articles about east London history. She tragically died in 2010 from a sudden illness.

PRAISE FOR THE GOOD OLD DAYS:

'A world of hunger, squalor, disease and pain' – *Daily Telegraph*

'Terrific. A delightful foray through nineteenth century murder and mayhem' – *Spectator*

'Packed with shocking and tragic tales' – *Big Issue*

Also by Gilda O'Neill:

East End Tales

The Cockney Girl

Whitechapel Girl

THE GOOD OLD DAYS

POVERTY, CRIME AND TERROR IN VICTORIAN LONDON

GILDA O'NEILL

ENDEAVOURINK

AN ENDEAVOUR INK PAPERBACK

First published by Viking in 2006

This paperback edition published in 2017
by Endeavour Ink

Endeavour Ink is an imprint of Endeavour Press Ltd
Endeavour Press, 85-87 Borough High Street,
London, SE1 1NH

ISBN 978-1-911445-52-4

Typeset by Palimpsest Book Production Ltd, Falkirk, Stirlingshire

Printed and bound in Great Britain by
Clays Ltd, St Ives plc

www.endeavourpress.com

For John O'Neill

My thanks, as always,
to Eleo Gordon and Lesley Levene,
and to the staff of the Four Seasons Hotel,
Canary Wharf, who made the place our home
during a very difficult time of loss and bereavement

TABLE OF CONTENTS

INTRODUCTION

It is curious . . . supplying information concerning a large
body of persons, of whom the public has less knowledge
than of the most distant tribes of earth . . .

> Henry Mayhew, *London Labour and the London Poor*,
> 1861-2

. . . crime is a disease of our moral condition . . .

> *East London Advertiser*, 3 January 1863

The past is a foreign country: they do things differently there.

> L. P. Hartley, *The Go-Between*, 1953

*

At times of great change – such as, for example, the
Industrial Revolution of the eighteenth and nineteenth

centuries, the technological revolution of the mid-twentieth century and now the electronic revolution of the late-twentieth and early-twenty-first centuries – it is normal for the impact and speed of new developments to cause those living through them to become fearful, and to ask questions about the nature of the society in which they are taking place. Suddenly people start to talk about the good old days, when everything was so much better. They want to know what is happening to the world, why it seems to be going to hell in a handcart, and, worst of all, why 'they' are letting this happen.

It is easy to believe that the past was a golden age: the sun always shone during those long days of summer, children played happily in the streets and fields, while Mum was in the kitchen cooking delicious roasts that Dad would later carve at the table for everyone to enjoy. Afterwards, the family would gather around the piano, having a wonderful time singing along together, the girls with their bouncing ringlets, the boys in their cute little sailor suits. So what could be more delightful than a return to Victorian times, when Britain was at the heart of an unbelievably rich empire that was the most powerful the world had ever seen.

Dig beneath the surface, though, and the situation becomes more murky. Here is Thomas Archer, for instance, writing in 1870 about starving children in London and the efforts some made to ameliorate their plight:

There are few more painful sights in this Great City than that of the sickly and suffering little ones in the homes of the labouring poor; for even where there is no lack of maternal tenderness, the daily struggle for bread cannot reach to the provision of such food and drink as are necessary to restore the lost strength, or to build-up the feeble frames of these little fading creatures. Happily this great necessity has not been altogether overlooked . . . To many of those who dine sumptuously every day, and yet are every day attracted by the announcements of the bill-of-fare in the great restaurants, it would be a new sensation to learn where they might take their place at the best dinners in London. It is true that they would only enjoy them by helping to fill a score of little eager mouths – would only appreciate their exquisitely subtle flavour by regarding them as vicarious banquets; but if they would go and see the midday table where their little grateful guests assembled, and listen to the musical clatter of those thirty or forty small knives and forks, it would be, in the best sense, such a hearty meal as would give to plain fare a taste of heavenly manna for some time to come, especially if the cost of superfluous dishes were spent in adding another long table to those that are already spread. There are several of these glorious dinner-parties in various parts of London. As many as forty of them are held once a-week, under the auspices of the Destitute Children's Dinner Society, which provides a meat-dinner for a penny to the hungry little ones attending ragged schools. This association . . . is designed, however, more particularly for the hungry and destitute. The institutions which refer more particularly to children, who are neither absolutely neglected nor entirely destitute, are intended to meet the very cases where such help is in some respects most desirable, by providing good and nourishing food for sickly, puny, or underfed, and consequently dwindling children, whose parents are too poor to give them the only medicine that can prevent them from becoming diseased.

*

OK, so maybe you had to be healthy, wealthy and male to eat well, or a child who wasn't averse to accepting a charitable meal once a week – if you were among the lucky ones selected to enjoy it. But surely it was at least safer back then, not like the crime-ridden times in which we have to live now? Well, maybe this wasn't exactly the case either.

When I saw the London *Evening Standard* headline on 22 December 2004 which read SHOPKEEPER KNIFE KILLING and then followed the subsequent media hysteria about knife crime – some of it alarming to the point of panic-mongering – I was reminded of reports of the death of another shopkeeper that also took place in December. But that one happened nearly 200 years earlier – in 1811. The shopkeeper in question, Timothy Marr, died in what became known as the Ratcliffe Highway murders. He, his family and a shop boy were murdered in a particularly gruesome attack by an intruder, and twelve days later, not far from Marr's shop, a publican, his wife and their bar staff were also found dead, murdered in a similar way.

Stories in the press and the speculation that ensued had many residents of Wapping and the neighbouring areas acting as if they were under siege. Sales of weapons for self-protection and of wooden rattles for summoning the police soared accordingly. The prime suspect for the murders, one John Williams, hanged himself while being held in prison, yet still the crime went on to obsess the Victorians, and – as here – continues to be written about to this day. So vilified was the suspect that his body was carried on a cart from where he had committed suicide in Clerkenwell, past the sites of the murders, and then buried at the crossroads where Cable Street met with what later became Cannon Street Road – in other words, in unconsecrated ground – with a stake driven through his heart.

This link with our own fears led me to consider other possible parallels between now and earlier periods, and I was taken back to my own childhood in the late 1950s and memories of the dreaded 'Flannelfoot'. Flannelfoot was a supposedly almost supernatural and violent burglar who could break into any premises without being detected because of his ability to remain absolutely silent. This information had been planted indelibly in my imagination by some older children who lived in our street, and although my mother assured me that he didn't exist, that he was in fact a character from a book that had been made into a film in the 1950s, he still had the power to keep me awake for many fear-filled hours. I listened – I suppose stupidly – for his paranormally silent efforts to break in and probably murder me in my bed. Thinking about it now, I can see that in his narrative there are signs of an updated version of accounts of the alarming encounters between Victorian maidens and Spring-heeled Jack, a creature who terrified our forebears with his similar, supposedly magical skills, including the silence of his approach. But he had other frightening attributes too, including the ability to breathe fire and to leap great distances in a single bound. We will see more of this Jack later, as well as something of his notorious namesake, Jack the Ripper.

There are plenty of examples of genuine criminal activity, panic about crime and fear of the dangerous elements in society to be found throughout the book. These cannot help but reinforce the view that perhaps the good old days weren't that good after all – especially if you were poor and from the labouring classes. What's more, they make us realize that such things are definitely not phenomena peculiar to our own modern times. Yet during the Thatcher years we started to hear the now famous – and oft-repeated – call for a return to the values of Victorian times, when, as we will see, the age of consent was twelve years old, child abuse was a matter of national concern and the lower strata of society lived in unimaginably vile conditions, a harsh, daily reality that can barely be imagined. The conditions were so bad that lists of official 'nuisances' that could warrant police or court action were compiled. According to Charles Dickens's son in his *Dictionary of London*, these nuisances could include anything from discharging firearms to retaining an infectious dead body in a room where persons were living; from selling disease-infected clothes and bedding to keeping a disorderly house – with plenty of horrors in between. Hardly a time or place to which any right-thinking person would wish to return. Who, for example, would be attracted by the thought of whole families dwelling close to the Thames making their living from toshing? This occupation involved going down into the primitive sewerage systems that emptied out straight into the river. Once there the families would sieve through the mud, excrement and filth to see what they could find. Some even made a reasonable living from selling items such as pieces of jewellery that had dropped down drains in the streets above. With the widespread lack of household plumbing and washing facilities, and the overcrowded slum living conditions in the areas in which the toshers dwelt, we, with our hot and cold running water, soaps and deodorizing sprays, can only imagine what their neighbours must have thought of them. But then they probably didn't smell too sweet either.

It wasn't only the people living in such squalor who caused the general stench that pervaded the streets. When he went to investigate living conditions in the East End, Thomas Beames reported the following reasons for the vile stink that filled the air in just one very small London parish: 'Fourteen cow sheds, two slaughter houses, three boiling houses [of bones for glue], seven bone stores'. Smaller animals would live with their owners in their room, but even larger animals, such as cows and horses, were kept alongside human residents in makeshift lean-to-type buildings and basements. They produced gallons of liquid waste and manure but their stalls had no mechanism for drainage, and as their feed was stacked alongside them by the dung heaps and soiled bedding, it is no surprise that milk became so easily contaminated and that disease was so easily spread.

Many of the slaughterhouses around Whitechapel and Aldgate were below ground and terrified herds of beasts would be a regular sight as they were driven through the dung-slicked streets that were already swarming with horse traffic, handcarts and pedestrians. With such sights, sounds and smells being commonplace, it is little wonder that investigators looking in to conditions in east London commented on the almost nonchalant cruelty they witnessed in even the youngest of children, who would jostle with each other to get a better view of the animals being slaughtered with a perfunctory wallop of the pole-axe. Philanthropists such as Canon Samuel Barnett called for an end to such practices, which he believed could only add further to the brutalization of a people already numbed by the harshness of their environment. But his was an uphill task, when people were more concerned with struggling to achieve the most basic of living conditions for themselves, against a background of cholera epidemics that were sweeping the country as the problem of waste disposal increased in line with the rapidly expanding Victorian population.

Waste had been dealt with in earlier periods simply by dumping it in open gullies, but then a system had been introduced in which open cesspits were built under dwellings. These basement holes were allowed to fill until they were overflowing with excrement, at which point, eventually, they were emptied and the daintily named 'night soil' could be taken away – at a cost – to the east, to fertilize the fields and market gardens of Essex. But as the pressure to build more houses and places of manufacture grew in the city, the burgeoning urbanization was to see the end of the rural idyll on the other side of the River Lea. With the absence of land to fertilize, the problem of what to do with all that waste, both human and animal, returned, creating perfect conditions in which cholera could flourish.

Surprisingly, it wasn't only in the poorer neighbourhoods that such disgusting and unhygienic conditions prevailed. Mrs C. S. Peel's *Homes and Habits*, reproduced in G. M. Young's book on Victorian England, has the following unpleasant insight into the homes of the wealthy, although it would seem that they weren't the ones to suffer as a result.

As late as 1844 no less than fifty-three overflowing cesspits were discovered under Windsor Castle, and later still at a north country mansion attention was drawn to an old cesspool . . . giving way as a carriage pulled up to the second front door, which led from a back hall into the stable yard on to which the service premises looked. It is true that footmen who used the pantry sink often had sore throats, but it was not until the earth opened and partly engulfed the carriage that the cause of their illness was discovered.

In 1847, out of a desperation combined with ignorance, cesspits were banned, but as there was nothing to take their place it was only a matter of time before disaster struck. Rubbish was deposited in any available sewers and streams, which in turn decanted their filth into the Thames. The result was that by the 1850s Victorian Londoners saw their great river transformed – it was now a disease-ridden open sewer flowing through the city. But it needed the record heat of the summer of 1858 for any action to be taken to deal with the problem. This was the year of the 'Great Stink', when even the Houses of Parliament were affected. So bad was the smell that drapes soaked in lime chloride were hung at the windows, and carbolic acid and chalk were thrown into the water in an attempt to make the air fit to breathe. They didn't work, and it wasn't until Joseph Bazalgette was appointed to create his massive sewerage system that the problem even began to be addressed.

That said, considering another of the sometimes surprising and often unsavoury parallels we will encounter, we can hardly be complacent. The Victorian sewerage system still exists today and, as I write, anglers, sailors and other leisure users of the Thames are being warned that raw sewage is pumped into the river at the shocking rate of between fifty and sixty times a year. This is because the infrastructure – being both old and built for a much smaller number of users – is now unable to cope with anything much more than average rainfall. Anything more torrential and the flood drains spew filth into the water.

It isn't only the parallels with the modern world that I find shocking. Until quite recently I had thought that yearnings for a return to Victorian values had disappeared along with the end of Margaret Thatcher's influence within the Conservative Party, but while taking part in a radio broadcast I was surprised when another contributor called for exactly that. His demand – which is a better description – came as a response to the tragic death by stabbing of a fourteen-year-old schoolboy and the understandable media interest in the case. But the interest soon led to something more like a media frenzy than a reasoned debate on what should be done about the problem of youths carrying knives. The appalling event was held up as an example of one of the main crises of our times – yes, we really were going to hell in that handcart. Youngsters were no longer under society's control and hoodie-wearing hoodlums were controlling our streets. In fact, according to some reports, murder and mayhem abound on just about every street corner and we'd all better barricade ourselves indoors or pay the price.

As disturbing and heartbreaking as that young boys death unquestionably is, can we really say it is a result of 'our times'? Have we degenerated so badly? Or is it a sad fact that, far from having invented so much that is wrong with the world, we have inherited the ways of another age and then reinvented them in our own not very pleasant image?

I think that this is the case. Which is why I hope to show that hooliganism, fear of street crime and violence are not new, and that debates surrounding the breakdown of the family and the community were being well rehearsed even during the supposedly more orderly reign of Queen Victoria. Rather than beating ourselves up, we should be asking why such things happen, and then maybe we can begin to address our own contemporary problems in ways relevant to us instead of longing for a return to some mythical past.

Anyone living through even part of Queen Victoria's time on the throne would have experienced vastly different economic, social and political circumstances, with periods of war and peace, feast and famine, and a move from rural to urban living that was to happen alongside an almost overwhelming increase in population. In other words, the changes were easily as alarming, eye-boggling and frightening as those happening in our own time.

The move away from rural living was one of the most truly dramatic changes, with the 1851 census showing that for the first time in our history there were as many people living in urban areas as there were in the countryside. With people from both Britain and abroad being drawn to the opportunities – some realistic, some illusory – to be found in the mushrooming towns and cities, congestion quickly became a major issue. As can be seen in the images conjured up by Dore's illustrations and Dickens's writings of a cramped, fog-bound, rat-infested city, London was soon suffering from chronic housing shortages, and the already overstretched housing stock rapidly degenerated into multi-occupancy, insanitary slums. In addition to this, there was also the problem of growing competition for what was often seasonal or casual work. This led inevitably to low wages, poverty, the threat of the despised workhouse and a desperation that would see many turn to crime as the only means by which they could survive. Even if youngsters did find work, it was a common practice to employ them while they could be classed as cheap unskilled labour and then to sack them as soon as they reached the age when they could expect to be paid an adult wage. Finding a way to earn money could be so difficult that, in some circumstances, if adults didn't turn to petty crime to bring food to their mouths and the mouths of their children, there would be tragic results. A report in the *East London Advertiser* tells the following brief but heartbreaking story:

A young widow, Harriet Pinks was discovered unconscious and starving in her room at 6 St Thomas's-Road, Bow-common. A [four-day-old] dead baby was by her side. The surgeon attending revived her by placing her on a mattress by the fire, but nothing could be done for the child. It had died from starvation [even though well developed] when the woman had become unconscious . . . She was given supplies and the sympathy of parochial authorities who planned to remove her to the workhouse.

In some of the many other stories that show the harsh reality of life in Victorian times I have used evidence and examples from around the country as a whole, but the main focus of the book is always on London, particularly its East End. The main reason for this is that I am regularly told that the East End is 'not like it used to be'. This was a view I wanted to consider in some depth. Could it really be true that the East End had changed so much? Being a place of immigration, and as a result having a constantly shifting population, surely it has never been 'like it used to be'? But paradoxically, it could be argued that on one level this means it has always been the same. How can this be so?

The East End was, and still is, a place of arrival for immigrants, an entrepôt that has offered work in the docks and allied trades, or in the stink industries that grew up downriver – and so downwind – from the cockneys' posher neighbours, on the other side of what may have become a metaphorical city wall, but one that is still there nonetheless. And then there was the availability of low-paid casual work that could be found in the sweated slop shops of the rag trade. These were the Victorian equivalent of the present-day workshops we hear about that exploit workers in the Far East – though they also still exist in our own east London to this day. For the even more desperate, there was money to be made in the case houses, the notorious brothels brought to public attention by various scandals, the ultimate probably being that generated by the Whitechapel murders of Jack the Ripper. His victims were in some ways not so very different from the young women arriving today from Eastern Europe, who stand on street corners in exactly the same areas. Add cheap accommodation into the equation, the companionship of those from similar backgrounds – maybe even from the same village – and it is no wonder that London drew the crowds, and continues to do so. It is only the religions, languages and countries of origin that have changed over time, and for some – but certainly not all – the improved living conditions.

With Victorian London's open sewers, dark, forbidding alleyways and overcrowded slum courts, it is hardly surprising that areas like the East End were, on the whole, avoided or ignored by those with no business to be there. The exceptions included those 'going slumming' for entertainment and those who saw the inhabitants as objects of interest for social investigation or philanthropic intercession. But such intervention was, on the whole, insignificant and did little to stop the rookeries growing and festering, places where crime could – and did – go undetected, and which became the nurseries for new generations of felons. Makeshift additions were built on to existing rackety buildings as more and more people moved in, especially at times when other slums were being cleared for new roads and the railways. The rooms within these shanties were packed with people and their animals – everything from pigs and rabbits to chickens – and it was not only the rooms that were crowded. At night the stairways and landings would be sought out by those who didn't have even the few pennies needed for a nights kip in a common lodging house but weren't yet desperate enough to enter the workhouse.

THE GOOD OLD DAYS

As Thomas Beames described them, the rookeries were places where an almost sub-human species bred like the animals they kept there:

We may look, then, for a superabundant increase of the rookery class, with no corresponding growth of the industrious labourer, unless you check such increase by salutary laws, which strike down the nests, not where men, but rather human abortions, are produced. Grave may be the fears of the thinking man when he views the swarms of children who people the back alleys of London . . .

And Dickens, in his *Sketches by Boz*, makes them seem hardly more attractive:

The filthy and miserable appearance of this part of London can hardly be imagined by those (and there are many such) who have not witnessed it. Wretched houses with broken windows patched with rags and paper: every room let out to a different family, and in many instances to two or even three – fruit and 'sweet-stuff' manufacturers in the cellars, barbers and red-herring vendors in the front parlours, cobblers in the back; a bird-fancier in the first floor, three families on the second, starvation in the attics, Irishmen in the passage, a 'musician' in the front kitchen, and a charwoman and five hungry children in the back one – filth everywhere – a gutter before the houses and a drain behind – clothes drying and slops emptying, from the windows; girls of fourteen or fifteen, with matted hair, walking about barefoot, and in white greatcoats, almost their only covering; boys of all ages, in coats of all sizes and no coats at all; men and women, in every variety of scanty and dirty apparel, lounging, scolding, drinking, smoking, squabbling, fighting, and swearing.

As Dickens rightly noted, the majority of people did not witness such scenes, and men squabbling, swearing and fighting – even to the death – outside a slum ale house would be unlikely to attract the same official attention as would a similar event outside a gentlemen's club in St James's. If anything, a fine might be imposed, or the incident dismissed by the courts altogether. We see massive gulfs opening up between the lots of the upper, middling and working classes during the nineteenth century, and with the industrial innovations that brought wealth for the fortunate came the inevitable filth, contamination and environmental despoliation for everyone else. With every so-called improvement came further problems for the poor. As slums were cleared, whether from philanthropic or profit-making motives, and railways cut through what had been residential districts, where were the slum dwellers supposed to go? Some of the new housing developments, despite supposedly being aimed at the poor, fell far wide of the mark. They were often prohibitively expensive or were so highly regulated that the poor could not move into them even if they had been able to afford the rent, as they were prohibited from doing any work at home, such as taking in washing or doing outdoor work for local factories – common ways for the poor to earn the little money they did. So the displaced slum dwellers had no choice but to move into

the already over-populated poorer areas, making the congestion there even worse.

At the very edge of these ever-widening gulfs in human
existence there was an even more impoverished underclass,
a terrifying *demi-monde* of criminals, cheap tarts and no-hope
lowlifes, the layer of 'ruffians' who were being identified by
social investigators such as Charles Booth and Henry
Mayhew. Before his work began, Booth had doubted that
conditions could be quite as bad as had been reported, but
he soon admitted that he thought the truth was actually far
worse. Similarly, Mayhew's veracity has, at times, been
doubted. While it is true that his work is mediated through
a journalist's eye, we will see that there is so much other
supporting evidence that it is difficult not to believe that he
was recording what has been described as the 'reality of
daily life'. At the very least there is no denying that he was
the author of books that opened the eyes of comfortable
Victorians to the shocking poverty surrounding them.
Mayhew showed his readers that the extent of these divisions
meant that it could honestly be said by contemporary
commentators that the mores, the lives and even the language
of those at the bottom of the social heap were less familiar
to their wealthier neighbours in the 'better' parts of London
than those of the inhabitants of so-called 'darkest Africa'.

Geographically, there often wasn't that much distance
between the rich and poor, but in all other senses they were
occupying completely different worlds. As the Reverend
Harry Jones, who moved from a west to an east London

parish, wrote in 1857: 'My first impression was, perhaps, of the nearness of the East of London to the West. The East is, to many who dwell in the West, an unknown distant land. Anything beyond the City is infinitely remote.'

However, this unfamiliarity didn't prevent a certain amount of what might be called 'poverty tourism' – the aforementioned slumming for entertainment by those 'toffs' who chose to risk personal safety for the thrill of mixing with the 'roughs' in the taverns and music halls and to make use of the services of the prostitutes hanging around the dock gates.

In 1883 the Reverend Andrew Mearns, another social commentator concerned with the conditions of the poor, wrote in his *The Bitter Cry of Outcast London*: 'We must face the facts; and these compel the conviction that THIS TERRIBLE FLOOD OF SIN AND MISERY IS GAINING UPON US. It is rising every day. This statement is made as the result of a long, patient and sober inquiry . . .'

As with other commentators, including even the most sympathetic, there is an underlying feeling that if we don't do something fast about these people, then we will all suffer the consequences. It wasn't just a fear of the unknown that caused such worries. There is no denying that London could be a dangerous place. Uniformed gangs would 'hold their street' in violent clashes with opposing mobs; prostitutes would lure unsuspecting men into alleyways, where they would be coshed by the women's accomplices, the 'bullies' who waited in the shadows; even the Queen herself was not safe in the capital, with at least seven – some claim as many as eight – assassination attempts being made on the royal person. And then there were the fears fuelled by stories of foreigners jumping ship and setting up home by the riverside, close to the massive wealth secreted in the bonded warehouses – the skyscrapers of their day. With the perceived propensity of these 'alien hordes' for making a living from thievery, opium and whores, the Victorian East End was portrayed as a place to be visited only by the foolhardy or the desperate – or, of course, the louchely curious, who cared less about the danger than the thrills to be had. There are parallels today with the sorts of wealthy, celebrity pleasure-seekers who enjoy mixing with ex-gangsters or criminals.

The writer A. N. Wilson has claimed in his book *The Victorians* that even if we feel we 'still live in a world shaped by [them] there is another sense in which they have vanished totally'. He then goes on to talk about the lost oral tradition and lost physical details of the Victorian world. But I disagree with him. Those links with the Victorian age are still with us, and not just in the paintings and artefacts in galleries and museums, in the dusty, yellowing records of libraries and archives, or in the architecture of so many town and city centres. That Victorian London continues to exist in the speech of cockneys of my father's generation – children from the early twentieth century born to nineteenth-century parents. He still used cant words such as 'bunts', meaning profit made on the side from a dodgy deal, and baffling phrases from a backslang originally used by Victorian market costers to keep their trading terms and criminal sidelines secret from the general public – the mug punters with whom they did their daily business. He regularly used words for money and clothing that, though gradually being lost, remain with us to this day. And my grandmother told me stories about her childhood, when she helped my great-grandmother, who worked in the music halls around Whitechapel, and about how she met Marie Lloyd. Even in my post-war generation there still exist living memories of more tangible relics of Victorian times. I remember the elderly hawkers in Petticoat Lane in the 1960s, squatting on the pavements between the market stalls, with their wooden barrels of *heimische* pickled cucumbers and herrings, and beigels threaded on broomsticks, selling them just as their predecessors had done, when the streets would ring with Yiddish rather than the Bengali shouts and greetings we hear today. Up until a few years ago, on the corner of Sclater Street and Brick Lane, where the costers once sold their wares, an elderly man, dressed in clothes almost identical to those of his Victorian ancestors, would stand with a string around his neck threaded with gold and jewel-encrusted 'groins' – rings – and with rows of wristwatches worn along the length of both his arms. He would loudly berate the surrounding stallholders for selling fake designer jewellery, when his was the genuine, stolen item, and insist that they were destroying his trade. His place has now been taken by Eastern European lads selling tobacco and cigarettes of dubious provenance, keeping up the tradition of flashy herberts earning money by offering dodgy merchandise to willing, often gullible punters who think they are getting a sly bargain rather than merely inferior goods that are of little use or value. But the street markets have always had another important place in the lives of the less well off.

Living in multiple-occupancy dwellings, many had no proper cooking facilities and depended on the street vendors and food shops for their meals. There were, and still are, eel and pie shops – such as the one run by my grandmother – in most East End markets. And there were the fried-fish sellers who offered cold fish from trays hanging around their necks that were so popular with the Jewish community; it is from here that the familiar fish and chip shops evolved. You can still buy oysters on East End shellfish stalls today, just as you could a century ago. Then there were the pork butchers, often coming from German backgrounds, who sold pigs' trotters and spicy faggots that were supposed to be eaten hot but could be bought much more cheaply once they had gone cold – sliced up, they made delicious sandwiches. In my childhood, a stall in Chrisp Street market had stainless-steel vats steaming the faggots and the gloopy, yellow pease pudding that stretched the meal. But even the dullest of food could be spiced up with a bit of relish: those *heimische* cucumbers were a favourite, or a sprinkling of vinegar on the pies, eels and fried fish, or splashed over a brown paper bag full of steaming hot pigs' trotters. When I was interviewing people who had lived in London during the Second World War for a previous book, everyone who spoke about the plain food available on ration would delight in remembering that 'bit of relish' – anything from a splodge of mustard to a few pickled vegetables – that added to their pleasure. The tradition is carried on today in the chilli sauce and pickles offered in chip shops and kebab joints all over Britain.

Another tradition that has continued through the generations concerns the 'brides' or 'brasses' – the cheap prostitutes who plied the streets, favouring particular areas in which to work. In my childhood the top, westerly end of Cable Street was still a frighteningly rough place. It was dotted with the coffee shops in which the pimps – mostly Maltese at that particular time in the capital's history – would sit, sipping their drinks and smoking, while keeping an eye on their 'girls' as they tried to reel in the punters, in much the same way as was described a hundred years previously when that bit of the road had been known as Rosemary Lane.

My own and my family's memories and experiences therefore contradict the currently fashionable view put forward by some commentators who claim that much of what is written about the 'old' East End has been sensationalized and perhaps it was an area that wasn't so poor or criminal after all. But anyone can make mistakes. For instance – on a far smaller domestic scale – I have a little beaded cloth, which I drape over my cream jug, of the sort mentioned by Wilson as a Victorian article which no longer exists. I bought mine only last year.

Where I do agree with these writers is that then, as now, 'society' was, and is, being blamed by the better-off for allowing a dependency culture to develop among the poor. Regardless of the reality of people's experience and intentions, it was decided that the workhouse – a system introduced following the revision of the Poor Laws in the 1834 Amendment Act – should be a place that was dreaded rather than a soft option for the malingering idle. Yet in spite of this, the workhouse would be inhabited by all too many, including my own great-aunt Mog, who was given the privilege of being allowed out at weekends, still wearing her hated workhouse uniform, to stay the night with my grandmother in the chronically overcrowded rooms she and her family rented in a house in Poplar. While there was wealth for some that would previously have been unimaginable, the poorer classes were suffering, particularly in the 1830s and 1840s, and even the middling, business classes struggled during the economic problems that threatened to undermine the strength at the heart of the empire from the early 1870s to the mid-1890s. But this was misery of a different order from that experienced continually by the most disadvantaged at the very bottom of the economic scale.

Andrew Mearns went to look at the circumstances in which those poorest classes were living in London and described the conditions in the rookeries as being no better than those of the 'middle passage of the slave ship'. He thought that the individuals who huddled together in the outdoors under dripping railway arches were to be envied in comparison. He described how he entered the rookeries to seek out the mysteries of the inhabitants' lives:

> . . . *you had to penetrate courts reeking with poisonous and malodorous gases arising from accumulations of sewage and refuse scattered in all directions and often flowing beneath your feet . . . many of them which the sun never penetrates . . . You have to ascend rotten staircases, which threaten to give way beneath every step, and which, in some places, have already broken down, leaving gaps that imperil the limbs and lives of the unwary. You have to grope your way along dark and filthy passages swarming with vermin. Then, if you are not driven back by the intolerable stench, you may gain admittance to the dens in which these thousands of beings . . . herd together.*

He went on to talk about how each room was taken up by a family, and sometimes by their livestock as well – one having four pigs living with them in the tiny space. Elsewhere a woman was giving birth to yet another baby, while her seven other children and her husband, sick with smallpox, were in the same room; tragically, more than one of the rooms he visited had a dead child lying in it.

The conditions in which my father lived as a child were far from being so ghastly, but when I read Mearns the overcrowding reminded me of hearing my dad talking about the small terraced house in which he spent his early years.

I was open-mouthed at the time. How could Dad, Nan and Grandad, Uncle Billy and all the other kids have fitted into that space? The little terraced house was so small. They *couldn't* all have lived in there, especially when Great-aunt Mog was staying at weekends. 'Course we didn't, daft,' was my father's reply. 'We had the Harrises living upstairs.'

Affordable, decent housing was, needless to say, as much of a problem in the nineteenth and twentieth centuries as it is now in the twenty-first. And just like any other members of the poorer labouring classes, the inhabitants of those Victorian rookeries struggled to make a living, especially those who were ill or widowed, and who had to get by without the benefits of a welfare safety net, however inadequate or full of holes. Some did homework, such as fur-pulling and making matchboxes or sacks, while others went on the streets, selling anything from a few specky apples gathered from the gutters after the wholesale markets had closed to birds' nests, pigs' trotters and herrings.

Matchbox makers earned only a couple of pennies per gross for their pains, out of which they were expected to pay for their own paste and tools; as recently as 1904, there was a report in the *Hackney Gazette* of a Shoreditch matchbox maker who earned so little that the official reason for her death was recorded as exhaustion and malnutrition-induced disease. As for sack making, it was physically gruelling. Like matchbox making, it was always done as piecework, and the worker – most often a woman – had to wear a leather pad on her hand to help her push the big needle threaded with thick lengths of twine through the tough canvas. With the monetary return being so shamefully low for the huge amount of effort required to earn anything near a worthwhile wage, others were driven to try different ways of earning money. Mearns wrote about one woman he met who 'turns her children into the street in the early evening because she lets her room for immoral purposes until long after midnight, when the poor little wretches creep back again if they have not found some [other] miserable shelter . . . But even he concedes that the rookeries were still preferable to the common lodging houses, about which we will learn more later.

Other work that was carried out by the very poor, whether in London or other parts of the country, was either vile or dangerous, or both, with children as well as adults being expected to contribute whatever money they could to the household, and children really did work. Despite legislation to prevent chimney sweeps using climbing boys, this dangerous and cruel practice continued well into the mid-1870s, with householders more concerned that they shouldn't be bothered with the nuisance of chimney fires than with the welfare of young children. Sadly, because slighter youngsters were better able to gain access to narrower chimney spaces, some were as young as four years old. Appallingly, reluctant climbers would be forced up the chimney by their masters, who would do so by poking them with sticks or lighting fires beneath them. For similar reasons of size and agility, children were used in the cloth-weaving industry to scurry around under moving machinery to retrieve shuttles and bobbins, endangering – literally – life and limb. Children might also try earning a few pennies as crossing sweepers, dodging between heavy horse-drawn vehicles on crowded, smelly roads to ensure a mud-and dung-free right of way for ladies and gentlemen. Some of the descriptions used at the time to describe the children's occupation – shit-rakers and sparrow-starvers – probably give a more accurate impression of the work than does the bland term 'crossing sweeper'. Then there was the child employment to be found in the mines – pushing trucks of coal to the surface along rackety tracks, having to crouch and crawl through cramped tunnels far too confined for an adult. And goodness knows what dangers to their health were involved in pure finding – the collecting of dog excrement, which was then sold to the tanneries by the bucketload for use in the treating of hides. Almost as unpleasant was the work done by foragers, the individuals who made their money from human waste – everything from the lost and discarded items found by the mudlarks, or stripped off dead bodies by the rivermen, to loot raked in by the rubbish-tip scavengers and sewer toshers.

But, on the whole, for those who had little choice or opportunity within the legitimate world of work – and who didn't want to be condemned to the workhouse and its soul-destroying regime of pointless tasks such as crank-turning and stone-breaking – there was the temptation of all that wealth surrounding them. It's not surprising that there were those who turned to crime.

Most people who claim that they are starving in Britain today have no idea of the genuine hunger experienced by the truly poor. This was an opinion shared by Mearns, who was quite unusual for a Victorian clergyman in that, while clearly not approving, he had some sympathy with the poorest who ended up taking the criminal path in life. As Professor Lorraine Gamman has noted:

> *In law poverty has never been recognised as an 'excuse' for stealing, even in extreme conditions where people starved rather than steal a loaf of bread. In such harsh conditions the law breaker was rarely seen as a victim, but instead as a dishonest criminal [who should willingly starve rather than steal]. The pathologising, but nevertheless more liberal, discourses concerned with the mitigating circumstances of crime . . . that emerged in the nineteenth century, at first excluded the poor from their accounts . . . poverty to the point of starvation was not seen as a mitigating factor in theft.*

She also highlights another important gulf between the classes in regards to criminality, here using the example of shoplifting: 'It was usually the case that rich women were diagnosed as suffering from "shopping mania" while the poor were either transported or imprisoned.'

*

Queen Victoria's long reign lasted from 1837 to 1901. Those who lived during the earliest years of her time on the throne would barely have been able to recognize the Britain that existed at her death – a place that was on the cusp of the truly modern world. It is little wonder that such enormous changes caused fear and doubt. Even during the nineteenth century, historians and social commentators could not agree on whether the era was one of repression or permissiveness, morality or vice; on whether it was a great or a terrible period in which to live. There is evidence to support both points of view, but in the end, as was suggested earlier, it was probably like most places where people live today – not too bad if you were healthy, wealthy and male. It is this doubt that can speak to us about the uncertainties and insecurities that developed during the period, a time of astonishing economic, social and political change, which benefited some but denied even basic rights to so many This disparity was to cause moments of great alarm and fear, anxieties about which can be detected particularly clearly in accounts relating to crime, and a belief that there was a breakdown of 'civilization as we know it' happening right under people's noses.

In the following chapters we will see the sorts of crimes, immorality, scams and outright social disorder that an individual walking the streets at the centre of the richest empire ever might have encountered in the nineteenth century, and the parallels with life today will be startling. I won't keep pointing out every one of them, but I like the idea that you will be spotting your own as you read the book, and that should certainly help put things into perspective as you watch, listen to and read all the daily news and spin with which we are now bombarded.

1

STREET CRIME, JUVENILE DELINQUENTS AND THE GARROTTING PANIC

The children now love luxury; they have bad manners, contempt for authority; they show disrespect for elders and love chatter in place of exercise. Children are now tyrants, not the servants of their households. They no longer rise when elders enter the room. They contradict their parents, chatter before company, gobble up dainties at the table, cross their legs, and tyrannize their teachers.

Socrates (469-399 BC)

. . . the rookeries [rear] whole gangs of juvenile delinquents [and] send forth children trained adepts at wickedness . . . taught noiselessly to do their deeds of darkness.

Thomas Beames, *The Rookeries of London*, 1850

The Reason Our Streets Are So Violent
title of online article on youth crime in *Telegraph online*,
Shaun Bailey, 2006

*

As can been seen from the quotes above, youth has always been considered something of a 'problem', and in the Victorian period youth crime – in this case, that committed by the offspring of the poor, who either chose or were forced into crime – was seen as one of the greatest social and moral threats of the day In our contemporary media reports, when the children of the better-off are shown committing crimes, they are treated as lads and lasses displaying high spirits – as, for instance, in recent articles covering the behaviour of students from the London School of Economics who caused many thousands of pounds' worth of damage on a drunken rampage through King's College, London. Meanwhile, the notion of juvenile delinquency is very firmly attached to the children of the poor and usually less well-educated classes – currently identified and demonized as chavs, who, we are told, are leading awful, meaningless lives.

The same contradictions can be seen in Victorian accounts of young people's behaviour, but living today in our developed world, with its welfare system, social support and other safety nets, it is difficult to conceive just how much responsibility the children of the poor were expected to shoulder in the past. Youngsters either contributed to the family budget or, as happened to my mother in the East End in the 1920s, did not go to school very often because they were needed to look after siblings while their mother worked, often in poorly paid jobs doing heavy manual labour in local factories and breweries. It is hardly surprising that with so little adult supervision in their early lives even very young children became involved in criminal activity. Whether it was pinching coal from the back of an unsupervised collier's cart, lifting bolts of cloth from a shop front to sell on or stealing food from the grocer's to feed themselves, theft was rampant throughout the rapidly expanding metropolis.

The young thief was well prepared and would habitually carry a knife, not only for self-protection or as a weapon, but also as a tool of the trade. Sacks of dry goods on the back of a cart could be pierced, releasing a potentially profitable trail that was left ready to scoop up when the unsuspecting driver shook his reins and the horse pulled away. And boots hanging on display outside a shop by their tightly knotted laces could be swiftly released with the aid of a sharp blade. These were everyday, commonplace crimes, but there were specific events that added to the general furore caused by these young felons. These were made much of by the newspapers. One such episode concerned the supposed mini crime wave that occurred during the August Bank Holiday festivities of 1898, when the polices attempts to take control of events was strongly resisted, with a violent response coming from the crowds. So bad was some of this violence that the *Daily Graphic* described it as an 'avalanche of brutality which . . . has cast such a dire slur on the social records'.

Other press reports were less alarming, highlighting behaviour familiar to us today, such as drinking, shoving and general 'larking about', but the idea that decent people were at risk from these youngsters had been fixed in the public imagination. Consequently much was made of outbreaks of what was known then as 'taking up the pavement' – groups of over-excited young people barging arrogantly along the street as if they 'owned the place'. A famous, regular example of this in the Victorian East End was still happening in my parents' youth – the so-called Monkey Parade that took place, in their time, along the East India Dock and Commercial roads. Exactly as in the nineteenth century, the youngsters of the early twentieth century – as spruced up, suited and booted as they could afford to be – would bowl along the street, showing off to friends, with the boys bragging and swearing and both boys and girls eyeing up the opposite sex. In Victorian times there were even shocked press reports that some of the youths were whistling and playing mouth organs. A favourite prank of the Monkey Paraders was to surreptitiously pin a sheet of paper to someone's back, then set fire to it, alarming their victim for cheap amusement – the happy-slapping of the nineteenth century. Or they would dip the palm of their hand in soot and then warmly clap a friend on the back, leaving a grubby imprint on the unsuspecting victim, who would then have no idea why he had become an object of derision. On warm summer nights, lads would opt to leave the parade early and then jump up on to the tailboard of a cart for an illicit ride down to the canal for a strictly forbidden swim. But innocent as most of this sounds, such general messing around could have serious consequences, as an undated newspaper article I found in the Tower Hamlets archive, headed 'Evil Effects of Larking', demonstrated when an incident on a building site was described. Two young labourers were throwing things at one another, but unfortunately one of those things was a chisel: 'The sharpness of the tool caused it to enter a considerable depth into the back of the young man, who was removed at once to Guy's hospital, where he lies in a precarious state.'

From even a cursory reading of the Victorian press it is clear that all varieties of youth crime and the wild behaviour of young people were causing widespread alarm, and in his *The Seven Curses of London* James Greenwood could claim, when talking about the recently introduced horse-drawn police wagons, that so much crime was being committed, 'Black Maria is the only one that's doing a trade now. Every journey full as a tuppeny omnibus.'

And according to Walter Besant, even little ones were up to no good:

> *At ebb tide [the barges] lie in the mud; the men in charge go ashore to drink; the boys then climb on board . . . If the barge is laden with sugar they cut holes in the bags and fill their pockets, their hats, their boots, their handkerchiefs with the stuff . . . they get a halfpenny a pound for their plunder.*

All this was happening alongside other, less specific events that were causing concern, described merely as rough youngsters 'running wild' in the streets and generally scaring the hell out of those who had anything to steal or who could be intimidated merely by the presence of such gangs. Although these mobs might just as easily decide to ignore the temptations of terrorizing the respectable public and choose instead to fight among themselves simply for the sake of it, with the same tribal logic that is displayed by present-day football hooligans, or the Mods and Rockers of the 1960s. Territorially connected gangs would have 'free fights' involving sometimes hundreds of young men – and sometimes women – going at one another on any stretch of open ground that was convenient for the battle.

London papers have recently spoken with indignation [about certain street companies] . . . They are organized originally for local fights. The boys of Cable Street constitute themselves . . . into a small regiment; they arm themselves with clubs, iron bars, with leather belts to which buckles belong, with knotted handkerchiefs containing stones – a lethal weapon – with sling and stones, with knives even with revolvers of the 'toy' kind and they go forth to fight the lads of Brook Street.

There is some controversy over the meaning of 'toy' gun in this context, but there are enough recorded incidents at the time of the criminal use of revolvers to indicate that it might simply be referring to a small type of firearm – as in the usage 'toy' dog. This is supported, for example, by a reference in *The Times* of 20 September 1875, in an article about what became called 'The Whitechapel Road Mystery' – the Henry Wainwright murder case, which is described later in the book: 'The skilled examination now concluded of the mutilated remains of a woman discovered in the Borough appears to show that she was shot in the head with a "peashooter" – one of those toy-like revolvers which can be carried without attracting attention . . .'

There were also references to criminals bragging to investigators about how easily they could get guns, claiming they were freely available in some of the rougher common lodging houses, particularly those at the Whitechapel end of Brick Lane, the area also favoured by the cheapest of the 'brides' – the prostitutes who would offer a quick knee-trembler in one of the fetid alleys that led off the main drag. These were the sorts of women who would come to the attention of a much wider public as the victims of Jack the Ripper.

There was one bizarre newspaper report concerning firearms regarding a Mr Henry Pye of Tomlin Terrace, Limehouse, who was charged with the attempted murder by shooting of his ex-sweetheart Matilda Madlin:

When called, the prisoner made a very odd statement that was not explained in anyway – 'I beg to state that I have been in the habit of carrying a loaded pistol for sport after practising on the flying trapeze. Also that I did not discharge the pistol with intent to do any bodily harm.'

I have tried to track down more information about this very strange comment, but sadly I failed. Perhaps it's just too pleasingly strange to tamper with. However, I did come across many almost casual newspaper reports relating to gun crime, most of them brief enough to indicate that there appeared to be no panic regarding the use of guns and their ready availability, although one coroner did comment that he thought it worrying that a gun and twenty bullets could be purchased for as little as half a crown.

But whether or not an individual had access to guns, there were plenty of other weapons to choose from, and not only those described earlier. There were also steel-capped boots, razors, blades hidden away in the peaks of the 'uniform' caps favoured by the youth gangs, and fish hooks sewn on to jacket cuffs to swipe across unsuspecting enemies' cheeks. And knives, of course, have always been a terrible threat in street crime – as witnessed today, with the period of the 2006 New Year's celebrations alone seeing the stabbing of thirty-eight individuals in the capital.

No less frightening to behold than armed assailants or mass free fights, although with no direct threat to innocent passers-by, was the ritual known as 'holding the street'. Any group having enough swagger or bravado to enter another gang's territory would be severely dealt with – or would maybe do the 'dealing with' themselves. This involved nothing more than refusing another gang entry into 'your' territory, and the subsequent violence which then broke out. A more recent example of this aggressive custom was described to me by a man whose older brothers and cousins had been Teddy Boys back in the 1950s: they would 'hold the street' on their local estate, even blocking the way of potential intruders at the nearby underground station to keep outsiders off their turf. Similar activities are still being witnessed in British towns and estates and in American ghettoes and projects to this day, with self-identifying groups such as the East Ends Brick Lane Massive keeping their territory 'safe' from outsiders. As Sukhdev Sandhu, author of *London Calling*, described when writing about young Bangladeshi men in his review of Monica Ali's book *Brick Lane* in the *London Review of Books* in October 2003:

These guys are Cockneys by geography and in self-image too. Walls and bus shelters are daubed with gang names – the Brick Lane Massive, Cannon Street Posse, Stepney Green Posse and the Shadwell Crew – that recall how . . . knowing how to handle yourself has always been a prized asset in the East End.

So nothing much different to the scraps, and worse, that broke out between the gangs in Victoria's reign. But, mostly, the incidents that make an impact in the press are those, like their nineteenth-century counterparts described by Walter Besant, which actually result in someone's death, even though they often seem to begin quite innocently.

The local regiment cannot always be meeting its army in the field of glory (i.e. for one of the so-called free fights) . . . *The boys gather together and hold the street, if anyone ventures to pass through it they rush upon him, knock him down and kick him savagely about the head . . . the boys regard the holding of the street with pride; their captain is a hero . . .*

But if the event became more heated and got out of hand, what had started as a posturing gang brawl could see the tragic end of a young lad's life.

It wasn't only boys, however, who were capable of fighting to protect 'their' territory from outsiders. That girls were involved too is something I remember well from my own childhood, when I transgressed one of the unspoken rules of my estate and passed the eleven-plus exam. Wearing the compulsory and distinctive school uniform set me apart and thus made me a legitimate target for violence, just as surely as happened to the Victorian girls who foolishly dared to venture into foreign parts – in other words, the 'wrong' street.

Unfortunately these aggressive young women didn't always mature into wiser, more law-abiding citizens – as James Greenwood observed in *The Seven Curses of London* following one of his investigations:

It is no exaggeration to say that there are many hundreds of women of which she is a type [drunk and foul-mouthed] the daily and nightly business of whose lives it is to prowl about this delectable neighbour-hood, seeking whom they may beguile and plunder, and it is equally true that it is chiefly at the public-houses and drinking-shops that they mature their plans for robbery . . . the women who swarm to their bars, and their concert rooms, and their dancing saloons, have no other object in view besides that of 'picking up' and despoiling the weak-minded individuals who are so unfortunate as to fall into their clutches. These women are the mainstay and support of half the public-houses hereabout. They go out in search of plunder of nights as systematically as did the foot-pads and the highwaymen of olden times . . . They do not resort to one tavern or dancing room and there spread their nets . . . such a plan would be by far too slow, uncertain and unremunerative. It is as with every other kind of fishing, this 'fishing for flats' – there is never any certainty as to the particular spot at which spoil may most plentifully abound. There may be an equal spread of it from the Pickled Herring to Paddy's Goose [notorious pubs] or it may all have shoaled into one lucky corner; therefore it behoves all who would share in the take to be vigilant and on the alert. And vigilant they are. They pursue their investigations, these flashily bedizened [gaudily decked out] and painted prowlers, with as cool an eye for business as do the night patrols in garrison towns, who look in at all the taverns in search of drunken and skulking soldiers.

There were even some commentators who suggested that most of the garrotting gangs, whom we will meet later, thought to be haunting the streets of London were made up of women and girls, as they were able to get closer to their victims without alarming them – either because they presented no apparent threat or because they were posing as prostitutes. Women also pretended to be innocent passengers on public transport while targeting unsuspecting men on whom they could practise their pickpocketing skills, 'accidentally' brushing against them as the vehicle made its way through the almost gridlocked city traffic.

Or, more simply, they could steal luggage while people were concentrating on buying their tickets or studied timetables at railway stations. This is a crime with contemporary resonance in view of recent newspaper reports on how people should be aware that gangs are targeting passengers at airports as they fiddle around, panicking about finding documents and passports and rounding up recalcitrant children.

But females were also, of course, as likely – if not more so – to be victims of street crime as were men, and a few became the victims of some very odd criminals indeed. For example, there were strange incidents of young women having acid thrown over their clothes, apparently without motive, as this letterwriter to *The Times* described:

> Between 8 and 9 o'clock last night my wife while walking . . . from Regent-square to Gower-street, had a large quantity of vitriol [sulphuric acid] thrown upon her back by some person or persons unknown. She did not discover the fact until after she had entered the house and was proceeding to take off her cloak. On reaching her hands behind to pull off the sleeves, her hands came in contact with the burning acid. It was then discovered that a large quantity of vitriol had been thrown upon her dress, and in a few seconds the velvet cloak – worth nine guineas – and a satin dress – worth six

guineas – were destroyed in a manner that only made us thankful that her person had escaped, and that the outrage had been discovered before the acid had penetrated further through the apparel. As it was, it had gone through the satin dress to the petticoat below, and had burnt the heel of one of the boots. So far as one can judge, there must have been half a pint at least of acid thrown upon the dress, reaching from a little below the collar downwards and all over the back. Not long ago another lady was the object of a similar outrage while passing through Gordon-square about 6 o'clock in the evening – a large quantity of vitriol was thrown upon her back, and was not so soon discovered as in the instance of last night. In that instance a valuable shawl was destroyed and the clothing, almost to the skin, burnt through. The stays came in shreds, as did the whole of the underclothing . . . I immediately gave information of last night's offence to the police at Hunter-street station, where several instances . . . of the like outrage appear to be known. The superintendent said they had as yet failed to discover the perpetrators . . .

Less fortunate were the women who suffered – again apparently motiveless – attacks to their actual person, having their buttocks stabbed with scissors. One perhaps more understandable, if still bizarre, street crime was hair theft, which involved being crept up on by the felon, who would make a few swift swipes with a knife or a pair of scissors and then run off at speed to sell their swag to the traders in human hair. One such trader is described here by James Greenwood, although the man claimed that he had obtained his stock quite legally, purchased from young women who had cropped the hair only from the back of their heads, so allowing the bald area to be covered up by what hair they had left.

It was recently my privilege to inspect, and for just as long as I chose, to linger over the enormous stock of the most extensive dealer in human hair in Europe. The firm in question has several warehouses, but this was the London warehouse, with cranes for lowering and hauling up heavy bales. I, however, was not fortunate in the selection of a time for my visit. The stock was running low, and a trifling consignment of seventeen hundredweight or so was at that moment lying at the docks till a wagon could be sent to fetch it away. But what remained of the impoverished stock was enough to inspire me with wonder and awe. On a sort of bench, four or five feet in width, and extending the whole length of the warehouse front, what looked like horse tails were heaped in scores and hundreds; in the rear of this was another bench, similarly laden; all round about were racks thickly festooned [with hair]. Under the great bench were bales, some of them large almost as trusses of hay; and there was the warehouseman, with his sturdy bare arms, hauling out big handfuls of the tightly-packed tails, and roughly sorting them.

Apparently the most highly prized hair was 'yellow', particularly for the export market to Germany, but other hair was still very saleable. That explains why it wasn't only young women wearing their hair loose who were clipped so cruelly; horses' manes and tails were also targeted by the thieves. And the Victorian ladies who chose to wear their fashionably long hair in a chignon or bun were no safer. The decorative hair combs holding up their tresses were seen as more than fair game by young villains, who could snatch them and then race away from the scene of their crime to sell them in nearby pubs – the 'hot' mobile telephones of the nineteenth century. And there was no sentiment or respect for religion; orthodox Jewish women wearing traditional wigs to cover their hair would have to be on their guard to protect their headwear from potential robbers, who would whip them from their heads. The thief would then take off, disappearing into the myriad alley-ways of Whitechapel and Aldgate. The wigs were then disposed of in the East End's busy street markets in what had become a predominantly Jewish area following the influx in the 1880s of refugees fleeing the pogroms of Tsarist Russia.

Alarming as all this certainly was, there was also some sense of perspective about these outbreaks of rough and outrageous behaviour among British youth. In an 1863 edition of the *East London Advertiser* there is a story with the headline 'Juvenile Delinquency'. It tells the story of twelve-year-old Alfred Waller, who stole £2 from his mother and then used the proceeds to take two friends to Blackwall. Had he wanted to keep his booty, he should have been a bit more discreet; as it was, he was forced to give sixpence to a boy who demanded money from the three lads. But Alfred had enough left not to get downhearted, taking his two pals to a coffee shop where they enjoyed 'bread and butter, eggs, coffee etc; [they then] bought some air balls and let them off all at once, and then had a lot of nuts'. Sensibly, rather than sending the Blackwall Three to the House of Detention, where, it was decided, they would surely be corrupted by more serious criminals, the court advised that the boys' parents should 'take them home and punish them . . . in such a way that they would not forget it'.

There were, though, some youngsters involved in crimes that involved quite terrifying violence and they were given far more serious punishment than that meted out to Alfred. A report in the *Penny Illustrated Paper* told the unhappy story of an incident that happened in Liverpool:'[A] sentence of fifteen years' penal servitude was passed upon the youth Lennon, who recently stabbed his father and caused his instant death. Both were drunk at the time.'

It wasn't only youngsters, of course, whose tempers flared to the point where they lost control. Disagreements between neighbours dwelling in tough, over-crowded conditions – especially when, as above, drink was taken to excess – could rapidly escalate into physical attacks. Arthur Morrison, in his book *A Child of the Jago*, a fictionalized account of real-life criminality and despair in the Old Nicol rookery, an area bordered by the Bethnal Green Road and Shoreditch High Street, describes the casual violence that was the way of life in such slums. And it was a way of life that could still be described to me by older members of my own family who were born in the first and second decades of the twentieth century, not only from their own memories but also from stories told to them by those of their parents' and grandparents' generations.

One startling image from my family's memories of life in the slums, similar to Morrison's account, was of women fighting in the street. The phrase that at first puzzled me when I was told about it was one woman taunting another with a roar of, 'Come on, get your blouse off!' It had to be explained to me that the women having the fight might well possess just the one blouse, and they would rather strip down and bare their bosoms to their neighbours than risk spoiling their garments.

But shocking as it might have been to have gangs of youths, men and even grown women fighting each other, this was nothing compared to the threat posed by street thieves, who were prepared to use extreme violence some-times against their victims. Although there were those who used no violence at all, like the pickpockets who worked crowded areas such as street markets or race meetings – much as gangs today work busy places like Oxford Street. They could steal a purse or a silk scarf with such dexterity that they didn't need to use force, and anyway they wouldn't want to risk drawing attention to themselves by assaulting their mark and provoking a maybe violent response. The most these thieves might do would be to adopt distracting tactics, such as pretending to brush bird droppings from someone's shoulder – a tactic nowadays employed at hole-in-the-wall cash machines.

Similarly there were the opportunists who stole from street stalls and shop fronts. They would saunter down the street, the picture of innocence, and simply snatch whatever was to hand and then carry on walking along as if they had done nothing untoward.

Walter Besant, when researching his book *East London*, became familiar with the activities of such lads: '. . . a boy, long-armed, long-legged; his step is silent and slouching, his eyes beneath the peak of his cap glance furtively round; the stall is unprotected . . . the hand darts out, snatches something, and the lad goes on . . . unsuspected'.

The shopkeepers weren't always the innocent victims of the criminal, however. There were those who were happy to buy tea, sugar, whisky or other expensive goods from the dockers who had 'liberated' these items from the bonded warehouses. A common justification for such behaviour, still being heard when I was young, was that the companies who owned so much wealth surely wouldn't miss such a small portion of their precious cargoes, and anyway, they were bound to be insured up to the hilt. The shopkeepers would also buy goods from less organized thieves who had pinched the odd pair of boots from a shop along the road, or perhaps a watch from a 'shoot flyer'.

Shoot-flying was an aggressive type of pickpocketing tech-nique carried out by thieves who would grab watch chains and pull as hard as they could, hoping to get the watch as well as the chain. They would then 'shoot off' as fast as their legs could carry them into the nearest alley or side street, where they hoped to escape capture – especially important if the victim or a passer-by had decided to shout 'Thief!' or take up the chase. Even if the chain broke before the watch came loose, the thief could still get a good price for a decent chain, making the daring attack more than worth his while.

But then there was another type of street criminal alto-gether, the garrotter, a thief who worked as part of a violent gang. It has been suggested that some accounts of crime in Victorian London, particularly garrotting, were coloured by the fashion for sensational writing about the exotically sinister East End, and this has led to doubts about their veracity. But from my family's links to the area in the – admittedly late – Victorian period, it would seem foolish not to acknowledge that a *demimonde* did exist and that its victims, including some of the perpetrators as well as those unwittingly caught up in its corruption, suffered just as they do today. It is the existence of this world, known only to those with the least privilege and to those who were targeted by it, that led – and can still lead – to the criminalization of a certain type of person. This can be seen in the so-called garrotting 'panics'.

There were two major recorded waves of this crime – one in the 1850s and another in the 1860s – but there were many other incidents cited throughout the period. Interestingly, the stir caused in the 1860s really only took off once an MP, Hugh Pilkington, was attacked in 1862. This is very like what happened with the Harold Shipman murder case, and criminologists have argued that the many deaths were only uncovered and investigated seriously once social status and financial misdeeds became part of the equation.

It is difficult to know whether these 'panics' were responsible for less serious crimes being reported as garrottings, but what is clear is that officialdom was taking them seriously. Police numbers were increased, sentencing and punishments were made harsher – including the reintroduction of flogging – and Queen Victoria herself made a call for proper lighting in the inner-city courts where the majority of the criminals were presumed to lie in wait for their victims. A piece in *The Times* of 18 January 1867 describes in horrible detail the flogging of two men convicted of 'garrotte robberies'. The punishment was meted out to them in the gaol yard before the commencement of their sentences of 'penal servitude' in conditions so harsh that they cannot but indicate the seriousness with which the crime was viewed by the judiciary at the time.

It is probably easier to dismiss such reactions as panic when you and yours are not the victims, but once you become the target things assume a very different hue. The *East London Advertiser* took the matter very seriously and on 3 January 1863 it carried the following piece, trying to work out what might be happening with the sudden upsurge in this one particular offence:

> . . . the *'dangerous classes'* are found more prone at certain periods to one phase of evil doing than another. Whether it be the imitative propensities of our species will of themselves furnish a solution, or that the phenomena are attributable to laws, hitherto occult, regulating crime like the atmospheric agencies which influence plague

and pestilence. The fact remains indubitable that we find now quite a glut of secret poisonings, now of burglaries, now of forgeries, now of incendiaries, and so forth. By this rule, garrotting is assuredly to be considered the type-offence of these days, for to this mode of assault, murderous as it is dastardly, our scoundrels most especially devote their energies. The whole press, with the Thunderer of Printing House Square at its head, has been no less loud and energetic in denouncing a state of things so dangerous to the public safety, than industrious in seeking for causes and remedies alike.

The manner in which the 'dangerous classes' were written about is reminiscent of how the ASBO – antisocial behaviour order – classes are now described, while reactions to their behaviour are reminiscent of the notorious events following knee-jerk 'devil dog'-type legislation, when laws were introduced, in retrospect too rapidly, to deal with the brutal canines that were about to savage all our children. This is what makes it difficult to assess whether the modern view that garrotting was nothing more than a panic is correct or if it was a genuine crime wave that people had every reason to take seriously As Rob Sindall has pointed out in his book *Street Violence in the Nineteenth Century*, the episodes can be fitted neatly into the pattern suggested by Stanley Cohen in his 1972 work *Folk Devils and Moral Panics*, with the media whipping up and dictating public 'panic', but I don't think that this invalidates the view that these crimes were genuine. Similarly, the individuals who were attacked by the garrotting gangs were not responding to a panic but were the victims of a brutal, specialized crime.

What made garrotting different from other types of violent street robbery – muggings, as they had become known by the 1970s – was how it was carried out. There were variations in reports of the incidents, but usually there would be two or three involved in the trap – one or two serving as the diversion and the lookout, while the other assailant would creep up from behind and put the victim in a headlock. Then either pressure would be applied to the victim's throat to subdue him or a weapon would be used to cosh him into submission. It came to be known in street slang as 'stringing someone up' and seemed to be particularly prevalent around the docks, probably because drunken sailors fresh off their boats with pockets full of wages made such easy targets for the gangs. But, as seen with the episode involving Hugh Pilkington, MP, it wasn't only confined to rougher areas, and in a letter to *The Times* of February 1851 another victim described his experience:

I trust you will kindly afford me your valuable assistance towards placing that portion of the public residing in the suburban districts of London on their guard, and also enable me to call the attention of the Commissioners of Police to the fact, that highway robbery, with violence to the person, is in this year 1851, likely to be as common, and, in consequence of the mode of effecting it, more easy and free from detection than it ever has been within the present century.

On Saturday . . . when returning home at night, and as usual walking quick, I was, without any warning, suddenly seized from behind by some one, who, placing the bend of his arm to my throat, and then clasping his right wrist with his left-hand, thereby forming a powerful lever, succeeded in effectually strangling me for a time, and rendering me incapable of moving or even calling for assistance, although there was plenty at hand, whilst a second easily rifled me of all he could find. I was then violently thrown on the ground, or rather I found myself lying there when I came to my senses. Two passers by, one a neighbour, raised me up, when we were immediately joined by a policeman, and by two more in less than a minute; but as I could not express myself coherently at first, the men had plenty of time to escape, and pursuit was impossible. I believe the approach of these persons disturbed the men, for they did not get all I had about me, and I escaped the finishing rap on the head usual in these cases.

Regardless of how many incidents of garrotting actually took place, there was a mass dread of being violently mugged by these gangs of stranglers which was certainly whipped up by popular newspapers – in a manner so familiar from the various frenzies encouraged by our modern tabloids. Psychologists have identified what they call 'floating anxiety', something to which whole groups of people, even whole nations, can attach their sometimes irrational fears. When there is no genuine threat – such as would be experienced in wartime, say, or during a disease epidemic – other enemies are sought and focused on. For example, when the 'Red Threat' from behind the Iron Curtain disappeared with the collapse of the old Communist bloc, other 'evils' had to be found to take its place. Currently we have Islamophobia stepping forward to fill the gap.

Victorian newspapers and journals carried letters, articles, editorials and cartoons all concerned with the crime of garrotting, which became known popularly as 'putting on the hug', with one correspondent to *The Times* suggesting it would more appropriately be known as 'putting on the Thug'. Thus the practice was likened to that of the Thuggees, the Indian gangs made up of cult followers of the fearsome Hindu goddess of terror and destruction, Kali. These gangs ritually strangled their victims, robbing them and offering part of their plunder to their many-armed, skeleton-adorned deity. In the 1830s the Governor General of India, Lord Bentinck, did his best to stop this centuries-old practice, and it was estimated that he and the anti-Thuggee campaigner Sir William Sleeman were responsible for the hanging of between 4,000 and 7,000 members – or alleged members – of the cult. Just the sort of chap, roared the editorials, that the streets of London could have done with to get rid of the garrotters.

But in the way that some present-day newspapers remind us to keep calm in the face of such alarms, *Punch*, while still acknowledging the problems and reality of violent street robbery, did its bit to mock the more hysterical parts of the uproar. Following the same reasoning as the street gangs and ne'er-do-wells who favoured clothes that drew attention to their tough status, the periodical suggested that potential victims might take sensible precautions to protect themselves and their wealth by wearing distinctive clothing – in their case, designed for crime prevention rather than gang identification. This included vast crinoline-type tailcoats to keep the garrotters from being able to reach the throats of their intended victims and viciously spiked collars to deter their nasty strangling hands. The idea was also put forward that decent folk might walk the streets of their previously safe world in a back-to-back fashion, the better to keep a lookout for unwelcome assailants.

Intriguingly, the spiked collars were actually manufactured and were advocated by some sections of the press as being a sensible method of self-protection – even while *Punch* was ridiculing the things in its cartoons. *Punch* also concurred with the newspapers that were calling for people to arm themselves to the teeth with revolvers, sabres, knuckle-dusters and blunt, heavy instruments in order to retaliate.

The idea of clothes designed for crime prevention isn't in fact so strange. Design Against Crime – a group based at the University of the Arts in London and headed by Professor Lorraine Gamman – is now doing exactly that with great success. In a mood that more closely resembles the jocular suggestions in Victorian editions of *Punch*, a recent letter to *The Times* of 28 December 2005 makes the suggestion that in our risk-fearing and avoiding twenty-first century the donning of body armour would 'reduce our chances of a random mugging' as we walk the mean streets of our cities and towns.

But then, as now, crime wasn't only committed within the confines of the criminals' own neighbourhood slums, or in the nearby 'posher' areas with their rich pickings; some rough types took the initiative by going off on criminal away-days.

Walter Besant describes one adventurous, if ultimately unsuccessful, group of young men who did just that:

> . . . *half a dozen of them thought it would be a good thing . . . to attend Epsom races on the Derby Day . . . the more glorious way [being] to go by road, as the swells go . . . These boys thought to emulate [them] . . . They helped themselves to a bakers horse and light cart, and, all in the gray of the morning, drove the whole way in the greatest glory to the race-course. Arrived there they sold the horse and cart to a Gipsy for three pounds, and spent the day in watching the races, in betting on the events, and feasting . . .*

They seemed to have enjoyed their excursion, but were not very successful in their criminal deceit and were arrested and charged that same day.

There were also, just as today, crimes committed by the already well off. One such was the Great Train Robbery. Not the one that took place in 1963 and became an iconic crime of the twentieth century, but the one that was carried out over a century earlier, in May 1855. The conspirators got away with gold bullion and coins valued at £12,000 – worth over one and a half million pounds in today's money It was only when one of them, Edward Agar, was framed for forgery by the previous lover of his young mistress, Fanny Kay, that the criminals responsible were brought to account. When he was sentenced to transportation for the trumped-up crime, Agar wanted Fanny to have his share from the bullion robbery and entrusted Pierce, one of his fellow robbers, to pass it on to her. When Pierce failed to carry out his promise, Agar, wanting revenge, turned informant and the whole gang was arrested.

So crime was being carried out by all types and in all areas, but how could this be going on in such a supposedly well-behaved and scrupulously prim and proper time as Queen Victoria's reign?

2

YOUTH CRIME, LOW ENTERTAINMENT AND OTHER ALARMS

. . . it chanced to me to visit a penny gaff in that dark and dolorous region, the New Cut. There the company and the entertainment were of a much lower character. A great part of the proceedings were indecent and disgusting, yet very satisfactory to the half grown girls and boys present. In the time of the earlier Georges we read much of the brutality of the lower orders. If we may believe contemporary writers on men and manners, never was the theatre so full — never was the audience so excited — never did the scum and refuse of the streets so liberally patronise the entertainment as when deeds of violence and blood were the order of the night. This old savage spirit is dying out, but in the New Cut I fear it has not given way to a better one.

J. Ewing Ritchie, *Here and There in London*, 1859

*

Today we want to know not only why there appears to be so much crime but also what are its causes. Unsurprisingly, now we are beginning to see the many similarities with the situation of our Victorian forebears, so too did they Why, they wondered, was there all this rough, let alone outright criminal, shocking behaviour blighting their otherwise increasingly wonderful world? Bad parenting – particularly mothering – and too much freedom were seen as obvious reasons, especially for youthful bad behaviour and crime.

According to Walter Besant, all delinquency could be put down to this wanton laxity and lack of supervision:

> *It is, of course, the old story – the abuse of liberty. We shorten the hours of work, and we offer nothing in [its] place . . . except the street . . . They begin by walking about in little companies [smoking] cheap cigarettes, called, I believe, 'fags' . . . they occupy a great deal of pavement, they hustle each other, regardless of other people; they get up to impromptu fights . . . they make rushes among the crowd; they push about the girls of their own age, who are by no means backward in appreciating and returning these delicate attentions; they whistle and sing, and practise the calls of the day and the local locality.*

But there was also a school of thought believing that rough and criminal behaviour came about as a direct result of young people being influenced by low entertainments. The penny gaffs and less salubrious music halls were condemned as having a corrupting effect, in much the same way as violent 'video nasties', DVDs and computer games have been blamed more recently. It was true that just as *Punch* was directed at a certain type of knowing readership – for instance, in some of its arch reporting about the garrotting gangs – so the 'penny dreadfuls' were directed firmly at the youth market, feeding an adolescent taste for gory tales of murder, highway robbery and piracy.

In his *Seven Curses of London*, James Greenwood described what he believed was the almost addictive nature of this corrupting literature and claimed that it might have the same debasing effect even on 'decent' youngsters:

[Does] all such coarse and vulgar trash find its level amongst the coarse and vulgar, and . . . gain no footing above its own elevation? It may so stand in reason, but unfortunately it is the unreasonable fact that this same pen poison finds customers at heights above its natural low and foul waterline . . . How otherwise is it accountable that at least a quarter of a million of these penny numbers are sold weekly? How is it that in quiet suburban neighbourhoods, far removed from the stews of London, and the pernicious atmosphere they engender; in serene and peaceful semi-country towns where genteel boarding schools flourish, there may almost invariably be found some small shopkeeper who accommodatingly receives consignments of 'Blue-skin,' and the 'Mysteries of London,' and unobtrusively supplies his well-dressed little customer with these full-flavoured articles? Granted, my dear sir, that your young Jack, or my twelve years old Robert, have minds too pure either to seek out or crave after literature of the sort in question, but not infrequently it is found without seeking.

It is a contagious disease, just as cholera and typhus and the plague are contagious, and, as everybody is aware, it needs not personal contact with a body stricken to convey either of these frightful maladies to the hale and hearty. A tainted scrap of rag has been known to spread plague and death through an entire village, just as a stray leaf of 'Panther Bill,' or 'Tyburn Tree' may sow the seeds of immorality amongst as many boys as a town can produce.

There was genuine concern that young heads were being turned by such material and that youth crime would soar as a result of youngsters imitating the lurid stories in these cheap instalment publications. It was obvious to the critics of the publications: boys would read them and then rob their employers, buy guns and run off to become highwaymen. Greenwood called them 'poison pen'orths' and thought them no less than 'gallows literature', full of 'hideous vices and passions', and listed titles including *The Skeleton Band, Tyburn Dick, The Black Knight of the Road, Dick Turpin, The Boy Burglar* and *Starlight Sail,* and then went on to condemn the publishers for the temptations they set before innocent children:

The daring lengths these open encouragers of boy highwaymen and Tyburn Dicks will occasionally go to serve their villainous ends is amazing . . . by way of giving a fair start to his published account of some thief and murderer, publicly advertised that the buyers of certain numbers would be entitled to a chance of a Prize in a grand distribution of daggers. Specimens of the deadly weapon, made, it may be assumed, after the same fashion as that one with which 'flash Jack', in the romance, pinned the police officer in the small of his back . . .

Similarly the penny gaffs were blamed for being little more than breeding grounds of thieves and maybe even worse, filling, as they did, young people's heads with all sorts of immoral and criminal thoughts. J. Ewing Ritchie described a performance he witnessed as being 'indecent and disgusting, yet very satisfactory to the half grown girls and boys present'. Greenwood concurred as to the age of the audience, saying that these were places that attracted a younger crowd, and offered no half-price tickets, as 'They are all children who support the gaff . . . these dangerous places of amusement.'

These makeshift theatres were usually set up in a temporarily empty premises such as a shop or small warehouse for a knock-down rent until a permanent tenant could be found. Garishly painted scenes would entice the queues of youngsters to hand over their penny admission. Depending on the showman, the audience might first be treated to a bit of a freak show as they filed into the improvised auditorium. Then came the show itself: this would have a variety of blood-curdling mini dramas, involving anything from throat-slitting robbers to brutal, wife-beating husbands, with every kind of nastiness in between. Musical interludes were presented by scantily clad – in Victorian terms – women, who by most contemporary accounts were more titillating than gifted.

The material in the performances presented in the gaffs – like those in the less respectable theatres and music halls – was seen as dangerous and demeaning, and the concentration of such large numbers of over-excited youths as a breeding ground for criminals, provoking Greenwood to urge the police to pay special attention to these 'hot-beds of vice in its vilest forms'. Although, if they had followed his advice, the crowds would probably just have turned on the officers.

Then there were those youngsters who didn't need penny gaffs to encourage them into bad ways. They were the ones who frequented far less rowdy establishments, although it wasn't so much the performances that attracted them as the opportunity they presented for extorting money. They were known as chirrupers and their dodge was to accost music-hall artistes on their way into the theatre and black-mail them. If they wanted an enthusiastic response, the lads would clap and cheer – for a price. But if no money changed hands, they would hoot and whistle, hiss and cheye-ike, and generally cause a commotion, so ruining the performance.

Condemnation of the penny gaffs was also extended to the 'freak show' elements of the entertainment. These would feature people with genuine physical disabilities and other people or animals made up to look as if they had them. But they could at least earn money – in the case of some, such as Tom Thumb, a great deal of money, and celebrity too – and performers and their impresarios occupied an important place in popular culture. This would last right up to my childhood, when my friends and I visited the travelling fairs with their booths displaying everything from bearded ladies to mermaids.

Although such entertainments displayed a seeming indifference to cruelty, James Greenwood, writing in the 1880s in his *Mysteries of Modern London*, thought that there had been some – if not enough – improvement in attitudes, although animals seemed to fare better than people:

> . . . *in these days, when we can boast of a Society for the Prevention of Cruelty to Animals, it would be quite useless for any ruffian to attempt to revive the once popular back-street spectacle, of balancing a young donkey with its feet tied together on the top of a short ladder, the resting place of which was the performers chin. We have grown too refined, perhaps, even in our back settlements, to regard with admiration and liberal intent the sight of a miserable mangy old bear made to 'dance' by having his toes rapped with a stick, being kept the while reared on its hind-legs by the ungentle persuasion of tugging at an iron ring passed through the gristle of its nose. Such gross barbarities are no longer in favour even amongst the very lowest classes, but there is room for further improvement still. As witness the performer who, for many years now, has been exhibiting in the streets of London, the tools of his craft being a bag of large-sized raw potatoes. The man is beyond middle age, and his head is bald, or nearly so; and all over his cranium, from the forehead to the base of his skull . . . there are blue bumps, and bumps of a faded greenish hue, and bumps red and inflamed, and his bald sconce looks as though it had been out in a rain of spent bullets. It is not so,*

however; it has only been exposed to a downpour of raw potatoes. He is well known, and as soon as he puts his bag down, and divests himself of his coat, is quickly surrounded by a ring of spectators. 'Here I am again,' he says, with a grin, as he takes off his can and exposes his mottled skull. 'Here is the old man once more, and he's not dead yet. You'll see a treat today, for my taters are bigger than ever they were before, and, what's more, they're Yorkshire reds, the hardest tater that grows. I shall do it once too often, there's no mistake about that; but I've served the public faithful for five years and more, and I ain't going to funk over it now. Here you are: here's a tater that weighs half a pound if it weighs an ounce. Chuck threepence in the ring, and up it goes.' And threepence is chucked into the ring, and up it does go, high above the houses; and the man with the mottled head folds his arms like Ajax defying the lightning, and gazes skywards, prepared for the descending missile; and presently it strikes him with a sounding thud, and is smashed into a dozen pieces with the concussion, and bespatters his visage with the pulp. 'Now chuck fourpence in,' says the exhibitor, wiping his eyes, 'and we'll see what we can do with a tater just as large again.' I don't know whether, on compulsion, I would rather witness [this] or stand by and see another modern street performer making a fiery meal of strands of blazing tarred rope, daintily picked from a torch with a three-pronged fork; or that other stirring spectacle of the man who lies on the flat of his back, while another places large stones on the prostrate one's chest, and cracks them with a sledge-hammer.

So it seems that youngsters were being enticed away from healthier pursuits by gross street performers and the 'low entertainment' of the gaffs and in the halls. Even if they didn't actually imitate the scenes being acted out before them and run off to become pirates and murderers, the mere fact that they bunked into the music halls for free, pelted the unfortunate performers with specky fruit if the production failed to entertain or spoiled the performance by 'chirruping' was proof enough of the manipulative power of the theatre for those critics who disapproved of the behaviour of such rough young people. The popular press also agreed that such low entertainment had a lot to answer for. But there were others who were more measured and thought that the answers weren't so easy to come by.

As we are again debating the rights and wrongs of rein-troducing the stop and search 'sus' laws, wondering about the effectiveness or otherwise of using ASBOs, and whether electronic tagging and prison sentencing can control the street crime that in some areas is getting out of control, so the majority of Victorians were at a loss about what could be done to control their own lawless youth and the threat they posed to an otherwise decent society. The inculcation of religion, ever harsher punishments and strict education were among some of the suggestions offered as solutions, but the ending of poverty itself and the introduction of aspirations other than criminal into the lives of the extremely poor seemed not to have occurred to very many of those who could actually have done something about it. Though there were honourable exceptions.

James Greenwood recorded the horrors he experienced

while investigating London's poorer classes in the 1860s. He described the 'hordes of small Arabs' and the various other street rakers he encountered, noting that:

In England and Wales alone . . . the number of children under the age of sixteen, dependent more or less on the parochial authorities for maintenance, amounts to 350,000. It is scarcely less startling to learn that annually more than a hundred thousand criminals emerge at the doors of the various prisons [and] are turned adrift once more to face the world, unkind as when they last stole from it.

On the whole, however, the view was that young people should know their place and accept their lot – in other words, not rock either the moral or the social boat into which they had been born and in which they continued to flounder. Even the simple expedient of educating this group was not popular with everyone. Critics today object to the idea of sending young offenders away to be trained in the armed forces, claiming that this will only produce fitter, more disciplined and therefore potentially more dangerous criminals. Similarly, their Victorian equivalents were convinced that the provision of schools for those so-called street Arabs would produce a generation of educated criminals, who could then go about their illicit business in an even more cunning manner.

At least the little toerags could be identified by their uniform. Today's belligerent British youth has adopted styles to intimidate the law-abiding population. Currently they favour low-slung trousers, the waistband hanging down below their backsides, imitating the look of American prisoners deprived of their belts and unable to hold up their denim jeans. Preferred headgear is a hooded top worn over a baseball cap, which in turn is worn over a thick net bandanna, in imitation of the look favoured in LA gang culture. In the same way, Victorian youth chose to frighten their elders with their own versions of threatening street style, although without the barrage of electronic media we experience today fashion didn't change as frequently as it does now and was more of an adaptation of what was worn by others of their class. Street gangs would wear the flat caps of the era, sometimes coloured according to their gang allegiance, a white scarf tied at the throat – what my father called a 'stook', possibly a corruption of stock – waistcoat, jacket and bell-bottomed trousers fastened with a big-buckled leather belt, in its most alarming version ornamented with elaborate studded designs, the better to injure potential victims. There was also a preferred hairstyle: close-cropped at the sides with a long, forward-combed fringe.

These gangs might steal and rob, but they would also attack one another in the violent clashes when they 'held their street' in the big territorial fights, as well as in smaller skirmishes – using their belts and boots, stones and bricks and anything else that came to hand as weapons.

The so-called 'swell mob' avoided styles which would make them stand out and instead imitated the clothes of their social 'superiors' – the individuals they preyed on –

the better to go undetected. An elderly lady cited by James Greenwood was shocked to discover:

> *They did not look like a thief, or a forger, or a stabber . . . 'Lord bless us,' I heard [her] exclaim, in the case of an oft-convicted scoundrel of the 'swell mob' tribe, over whose affecting trial she had shed many tears . . . as the jury found him guilty, and sentenced him to two years' hard labour, 'so thin, and genteel, and with spectacles on too!'*

It wasn't only clothes that distinguished the different types of young thieves, it was also the ways in which they went about their business. Mayhew identified those who were trained by professionals, others who were the children of professional thieves following in the family tradition and those who were so poor that they began their life of crime by stealing food merely in order to stay alive.

Similarly the thieves' targets differed. Horses could be sold on at a good profit, either as transport or, in the case of less valuable animals, to the knacker's yard for rendering down into glue. Dogs were also the focus of thieves' attention. In incidents like those current in today's news stories, there were Victorian individuals and gangs who specialized in stealing the pets of wealthy owners. The criminals would then either blackmail the owner with threats of what might happen to their beloved pet if money wasn't handed over or innocently accept any reward the owner had advertised in the newspaper for the safe return of the poor 'lost' creature.

It seems incredible, but by 1844 this had become such

a problem that Richard Mayne, Commissioner of the Metropolitan Police, was called to give evidence to a parliamentary Select Committee on Dogs, and he concluded that it was definitely part of organized crime.

There was another type who went in for dog-napping: the fan of the 'fancy' – dog fighting and ratting, both of which involved gambling for large amounts of money Cash betting away from the racecourse had been made illegal by the 1853 Betting Houses Act, after which all the off-course betting shops were closed down. This was to result in a new breed of criminal appearing, the bookie's runner, who would take illegal street bets and deliver them to the bookie at his house or pub, or other premises where he was based. And there were ever more ingenious games of' chance' being invented to feed the habit of the gamblers, many of whom favoured dog fights and ratting.

The stolen pet might be of a type that could be used to fight other dogs or kill rats, or it could be used for training and toughening up fighting dogs – by giving them weaker animals to attack and thus increasing their blood lust. Despite the law of 1835 which had made bull, bear, badger, cock and dog fighting all illegal, the practices continued illicitly. Ratting contests went on in many places, but the pits were often in public houses, with the famous pit in the Blue Anchor Inn in Bunhill Row actually being commemorated in a painting of 1850 which is now displayed at the Museum of London. It depicts Tiny the Wonder, a Manchester terrier owned by Jimmy Shaw, the inn's proprietor, who would store up to 2,000 farm rats in his establishment at any one time. Tiny might have been small, but he was famous for being able to kill 200 rats in under an hour. Some animals weren't as skilled, or as lucky, as Tiny, and the terriers were sometimes as badly hurt as if they'd been in a dog fight.

There is a link with my own family involving my father's late uncle, who was famed in the 1930s for fighting dogs – not pitting one dog against another in his case, but dropping to his knees and literally fighting the dog with his fists. This too would happen in a pub – after drink had been taken and enough money had been wagered and put into the kitty to pay for the 'entertainment'.

Illegal betting of another kind was carried on in the pubs around the Bethnal Green end of Brick Lane, this time on the quality of birdsong. The birds were trapped in the Essex countryside and housed in tiny cages, some to be kept by their captors but most to be sold in and around Sclater Street and Club Row. The East End tradition of keeping songbirds is a hangover from Huguenot times, and carries on to this day, with the area remaining a centre for the – illicit – sale and display of wild birds. A raid in 2005 made on a Bethnal Green pub saw nearly sixty police and twenty RSPCA officers involved in the arrest of a circle of men implicated in the trade.

It should be remembered that with all the frenzy about young people becoming involved in the world of crime – both then and now – and the possible explanations and causes of their behaviour, youngsters were also the victims of crime, just as children today are targets of mobile telephone thieves. In *Oliver Twist* Dickens described the 'kinchin lay'.

> 'Stop!' said Fagin, laying his hand on Noah's knee. 'The kinchin lay.'
> 'What's that?' demanded Mr Claypole.
> 'The kinchins, my dear,' said Fagin, 'is the young children that's sent on errands by their mothers, with sixpences and shillings; and the lay is just to take their money away – they've always got it ready in their hands – then knock 'em into the kennel, and walk off very slow, as if there were nothing else the matter but a child fallen down and hurt itself. Ha! ha! ha!'

Money wasn't all that such predators were after. There are many recorded instances of thieves, mainly old women, stealing children's boots right off their feet, the clothes off their backs and even the mangling or laundry being fetched or delivered by a child running an errand. Boots in reasonable condition always carried a good resale price, which is why the charities who ran boot clubs, providing footwear for the extremely poor, would punch a hole in the side of the leather so that pawnbrokers or other potential customers would know they had been stolen – not that the deterrent always worked. But any items stolen from a child, barring the most extreme of rags, could bring in a few pennies, and even the tattiest of clothes might result in some small return from the rag and bone dealers.

There was yet another type of criminal with which

Victorian newspapers could frighten their readers: the dreaded foreigner, especially one armed with a blade. The *East London Observer* reported many such examples. One letter to the editor of several hundred words is printed regarding the case of a Chilean seaman. Armed with two knives, the man stabbed a couple of English seamen who had reputedly 'offered the savage miscreant no provocation'. The Chilean was sentenced to four years' penal servitude, but the letter-writer demanded to know why:

> . . . *the wretch was not sentenced to transportation for life [as] he ought to have been treated as a wild and dangerous beast unfit to be at large again. There was not one redeeming feature in his case. He quarrelled with a disorderly strumpet, and swore he would butcher someone that night, and as the two Englishmen were quietly passing along, attempted to put his diabolical threat in to execution [and this only] a fortnight since a Spanish seaman stabbed an Irishman with a knife in Shadwell [and previously] on Sunday 20th there was the cold-blooded murder of an Italian seaman by a Spaniard . . . by stabbing him no less than seven times.*

As if all that wasn't bad enough, Londoners had to face apparently non-human terrors roaming their streets. One such was Spring-heeled Jack, a creature who terrorized the early Victorians. He was described by those who claimed to have seen him as being able to leap thirty feet into the air, to have eyes that glowed like hot coals, pointed ears and nose, and the ability to breathe flames. The first sighting was in 1837, in Barnes, but he had soon crossed the river to the East End, where he became notorious for terrifying and molesting young women. So frequent did the claims of assaults become that the Lord Mayor was approached to do something about the 'urban ghost'. A report in *The Times* on 22 February 1838 had the following account of one of the 'outrages':

Yesterday, Mr. Alsop, a gentleman of considerable property residing at Bear-bind Cottage, in Bear-bind-lane, a very lonely spot between the villages of Bow and Old Ford, accompanied by his three daughters [attended] Lambeth-street Police-office, and gave the following particulars of an outrage committed on one of the latter: Miss Jane Alsop, a young lady 18 years of age, stated that at about a quarter to 9 o'clock on the preceding night she heard a violent ringing at the gate in front of the house, and on going to the door to see what was the matter she saw a man standing outside, of whom she inquired what was the matter, and requested he would not ring so loud. The person instantly replied that he was a policeman, and said 'For God's sake, bring me a light, for we have caught Spring-heeled Jack here in the lane.' She returned into the house and brought a candle and handed it to the person, who appeared enveloped in a large cloak, and whom she at first really believed to be a policeman. The instant she had done so, however, he threw off his outer garment, and applying the lighted candle to his breast, presented a most hideous and frightful appearance, and vomited forth a quantity of blue and white flame from his mouth, and his eyes resembled red balls of fire. From the hasty glance which her fright enabled her to get at his person, she observed that he wore a large helmet, and his dress, which appeared to fit him very tight, seemed to her to resemble white oil skin. *Without uttering a sentence, he darted at her, and catching her partly by her dress and the back part of her neck, placed her head under one of his arms, and commenced tearing her gown with his claws, which she was certain were of some metallic substance. She screamed out as loud as she could for assistance, and by considerable exertion got away from him and ran towards the house . . . Her assailant, however, followed her, and caught her on the steps leading to the hall-door, when he again used considerable violence, tore her neck and arms with his claws, as well as a quantity of hair from her head; but she was at length rescued from his grasp by one of her sisters . . . Miss Mary Alsop, a younger sister, said, that on hearing the screams of her sister Jane, she went to the door, and saw a figure as above described ill-using her sister. She was so alarmed at his appearance, that she was afraid to approach or render any assistance.*

Mrs Harrison said that hearing the screams of both her sisters, first of Jane, and then of Mary, she ran to the door, and found the person before described in the act of dragging her sister Jane down the stone steps from the door with considerable violence. She (Mrs Harrison) got hold of her sister, and by some means or other, which she could scarcely describe, succeeded in getting her inside the door, and closing it. At this time her sister's dress was nearly torn off her; both her combs dragged out of her head as well as a quantity of her hair torn away The fellow, notwithstanding the outrage he had committed, knocked loudly two or three times at the door, and it was only on their calling loudly for the police from the upper windows that he left the place.

Another encounter with Jack had occurred two days previously, with the two Scales sisters being attacked as they walked home in the dark from their brother's lodgings in Limehouse. The young women were just passing Green Dragon Yard, they claimed, when a cloaked creature matching the description of Spring-heeled Jack appeared from out of the shadows, spitting his trademark fire, temporarily blinding one of them. Witnesses came forward to support their story, adding that they had seen him leap away from the scene with enormous bounds, actually springing high enough to land on a nearby rooftop. Further incidents were reported right into the twentieth century, with Spring-heeled Jack being accused of everything from clawing and ripping off women's clothes to kissing them aggressively, biting them and roughly grabbing at their breasts.

Various theories were put forward as to the identity of the perpetrator of these outrages, including the suggestion that he was the Marquis of Waterford, a man noted for his fondness of callous practical jokes and his declared contempt for women.

One genuinely non-human predator prowling the streets of Victorian London was a creature that had escaped from Jamrach's famous emporium. Jamrach was a supplier of exotic items and wild animals, many of them purchased from sailors coming off the ships at the nearby docks. He was notable, among other things, for selling a wombat to Dante Gabriel Rossetti – this when the poet couldn't afford the young elephant that had taken his fancy. This worryingly unregulated practice of sailors bringing home animals from foreign voyages lasted well into my childhood and my grandmother had a spider monkey that lived in her sitting room.

In his *East and West London*, the Rev. Harry Jones described a notorious episode in Jamrach's history:

I could indulge the whim for a lion at five minutes' notice. My near neighbour, Mr Jamrach, always keeps a stock of wild beasts on hand. Anyhow, if he happened to be out of lions, I should be sure of getting a wild beast of some sort at his store. A little time ago one of our clergy, who knows of almost everything going on in the parish, happened to remark to me that Mr Jamrach's stock was low. He had just looked in, and the proprietor said he had nothing particularly fresh then, only four young elephants and a camelopard [giraffe] beside the usual supply of monkeys, parrots, and such small deer. The wild beasts are kept in Betts Street . . . but the shop in Ratcliff Highway is always full of parrots and other birds . . . The selling value of wild beasts varies very much. You must pay about £200 for a royal tiger, and £300 for an elephant, while I am informed you may possibly buy a lion for £70, and a lioness for less. But a first-rate lion sometimes runs to a high figure, say even £300. Ourang-outangs come to £20 each, but Barbary apes range from £3 to £4 apiece . . . a disastrous and distressing accident happened in connection with this store of wild beasts. One of the tigers in transit escaped from his cage in the neighbourhood of the Commercial Road. Finding himself free, he picked up a little boy and walked off with him, intending probably, when he found a convenient retreat, to eat him. Of course, the spectacle of a tiger walking quietly along with a little boy in his mouth (he had him only by the collar) attracted the notice of residents and wayfarers. Presently the bravest spectator, armed with a crowbar, approached the tiger, and striking vehemently and blindly at him, missed the beast and killed the boy. The tiger was then secured.

In a slightly different version of the tale, inscribed on a bronze sculpture commemorating the event in Tobacco Dock, Jamrach thrust his bare hands into the creature's throat, rescued the child and then led the tiger back to the safety of his menagerie.

*

It wasn't only poverty, bad company, low entertainment, the fact of being a foreigner or a natural propensity for ferocity that fuelled crime, of course. There were those who actively chose it as a way of life, preferring it, despite the risks, to a harsh yet mundane existence working in manufacturing or casual labouring. In cases when there was simply no employment available – to reject or otherwise – rather than starve or go to the workhouse, prostitution would be seen as a choice, as we will see later. And, exactly as happens today, there was the criminal behaviour that came as a direct result of too much drink or other mood-altering substances being taken.

3

VICTORIAN SUBSTANCE ABUSE

. . . sustains and refreshes both the body and brain . . . It may be taken at any time with perfect safety . . . it has been effectually proven that in the same space of time more than double the amount of work could be undergone when Peruvian Wine of Coca was used, and positively no fatigue experienced . . .

advertisement for 'Wine of Coca', 1900

Though used as a narcotic, antispasmodic, tonic, stimulant, and anodyne, it is chiefly as a sedative that laudanum is so invaluable, there being probably no disease, class, or nature of pain or suffering in which this article has not, or may not, be employed with more or less of benefit. There is no drug or compound used in the practice of physic that, properly employed, is capable of affording so much comfort and relief to the patient, in almost every disease with which he is affected, as laudanum, for it may, by skillful combination, and a judicious adaptation of the dose, be made to exert any special or general action desired; and . . . in conjunction with nitre and antimony, [may] be depended upon for the cure of nearly every inflammation that can assail the system, and thus entirely set aside the use of the lance in those diseases which were formerly thought only curable by depletion and bleeding.

Dictionary of Daily Wants, 1859

*

The generally held view is that the use of any mood-altering substances, particularly to excess, is a way of escaping from the realities of everyday life, and for those individuals in Victoria's reign who did little more than struggle to survive from day to day and whose conscious reality was all but unbearable, that must have been so. But such abuse wasn't restricted to those who were suffering the deprivations that come with poverty. According to a recent House of Lords Select Committee looking into the use of drugs, J. R. Reynolds, Queen Victoria's personal physician, was an advocate of cannabis. He cited its efficacy in cases of alcoholic delirium and spasmodic asthma, believing it to be 'the most useful agent with which I am acquainted' for treating violent convulsions. It was also widely rumoured that Reynolds prescribed the drug for Victoria's dysmenorrhoea. But drugs that are now considered dangerous were commonly used for medicinal purposes and were legally available well into the twentieth century. There was widespread recreational use far beyond 'bohemian' circles', with public figures from

Gladstone to Florence Nightingale being openly enthusiastic users of laudanum, which is tincture of opium. However, perhaps unsurprisingly, the reaction to the use of drugs depended on who was using them and where they were being taken, and the same applied to alcohol.

James Greenwood called drunkenness one of the seven curses of London, and in *Low-Life Deeps* he posed questions familiar to us today about the wisdom of extending licensing laws, expressing his concerns about the apparently out-of-touch nature of those in authority:

It is now nearly twelve months since the Licensing Amendment Act became law, and the main feature of it – that which relates to the half-hour extension of the time until which public houses and beershops may remain open at night – was put to the test . . . [this] last-mentioned indulgence was never demanded, never urged as necessary, never expected by a proportion of at least nine out of ten of those to whom it was granted. A mere hundred or so of tavern-keepers were at loggerheads with the authorities, as to the desirability of keeping open their houses a little later than twelve o'clock for the accommodation of people who chose to patronise places of amusement from which the audiences were not dismissed until that hour, when the Home Secretary, by a device, as remarkable for its simplicity as for its boldness, solved the mighty difficulty.

The surest way of winning the affections of a people is to show respect for its homely, time-honoured traditions and maxims. The right hon, gentleman, who was doubtless aware of the popularity of the old English saying, 'what is sauce for the goose should be sauce for the gander,' shrewdly judged that he could not go far wrong if he cut the Gordian knot in which the publican's disagreement was bound, by declaring his conviction that what was good for the Crown and Cushion, in the Strand, was likewise good for the Three Jolly Tinkers, in Brick Lane; and that, to put an end to the vexed question, the shortest way would be to tar them all with the same brush.

Greenwood was most bothered about the implications of the changes, and decided to investigate further by visiting Ratcliff. He called the area 'one of the worst and lowest neighbourhoods in London', and was shocked that there were more pubs than there were bakers' shops. As he was pronouncing on the matter, he quite properly wanted to see for himself what effects the extra drinking time had had on local people. He didn't seem too worried about the better-off drunks who frequented the gentlemen's clubs, whose members, if they had had a few too many – or were even totally plastered – could go home safely and discreetly in their private carriages. He wasn't particularly worried about men in general at this point, but about women drinkers and how they treated their children:

It is generally agreed that the bane of drunkenness is never so hideous as when it is demonstrated in womankind, and no illustration of the disastrous effects of reckless indulgence in intoxicating liquors appeals to an audience with such telling force as that of the once sober and well-conducted female yielding by degrees to the terrible temptation until she at length sinks to the condition of a gin-soddened poor wretch, lost to every glimmer of self-respect, and capable even of starving herself and her children rather than forego her only remaining enjoyment in life . . . It is no novel narrative. Almost every day it is repeated in some shape or other in the newspapers; scarcely a morning passes but the 'wretched woman' herself appears at the police-court to answer for her misbehaviour . . . But, after all, she is not by any means the extremest exemplification of the extent to which vice and strong drink may brutalize and change the nature of a human creature . . . I would undertake with one cast of my net in the sea of infamy which flows between Ship Alley and Gravel Lane to bring to land fifty petticoated specimens, the least vicious of which, compared with the ordinary draggle-tail drunken woman of London streets, shall be of jet black, as it were, compared with mere grey . . . In language and manner she is as coarse as a coal-whipper, and the guiding principle of her shameful existence seems to be to make known her contempt and abhorrence of all that is modest and womanly.

Greenwood wondered why the extra half-hour should ever have been granted in such an area:

And what amount of compensating advantage can be shown to balance the evils for which in Ratcliff Highway and its neighbourhood, 'the extra half-hour' is responsible? There are no night factory hands, no railway travellers, no playgoing folk in this quarter of the town to whom facilities for obtaining beer or spirits, after twelve o'clock, would be a convenience.

In the 1880s, he could have paid a visit to Shoreditch and taken the short stroll from St Leonard's Church to Liverpool Street Station, as in that small stretch of road he would have passed no fewer than twenty-two pubs. Abstinence obviously hadn't caught on among the poor.

When describing the area close to his chapel, Andrew Mearns can make even those figures pale into insignificance. Yet, with his usual impressive empathy, he can still find compassion for the 'sinners' who frequented the many drinking places:

Immediately around our chapel in Orange Street, Leicester Square, are 100 gin-palaces, most of them very large . . . Look into one of these glittering saloons, with its motley, miserable crowd, and you may be horrified as you think of the evil that is nightly wrought there; but contrast it with any of the abodes which you find in the fetid courts behind them, and you will wonder no longer that it is crowded. With its brightness, its excitement, and its temporary forgetfulness of misery, it is a comparative heaven to tens of thousands. How can they be expected to resist its temptations? They could not live if they did not drink, even though they know that by drinking they do worse than die. All kinds of depravity have here their schools. Children who can scarcely walk are taught to steal, and mercilessly beaten if they come back from their daily expeditions without money or money's worth. Many of them are taken by the hand or carried in the arms to the gin-palace, and not seldom may you see mothers urging and compelling their tender infants to drink the fiery liquid . . . These particulars indicate but

*faintly the moral influences from which the dwellers in these squalid
regions have no escape . . .*

It was taken as a given then, as now, that alcohol was one
of the major causes of violence at football games – a sport
that has always had a reputation for provoking strong feelings – whether, as in medieval times, the fighting broke out
among the literally hundreds of players on each side or, as
in more recent times, the battles are between the supporters
of opposing teams, the soccer hooligans who fight one
another. Then there are the attacks against referees and
other match officials when they make the 'wrong' decision.
In the 'police notebooks' that were compiled by the
police-accompanied investigators whose task it was to gather
information for Charles Booth's survey of the conditions
of Victorian Londoners, there is a reference logging the
fact that Millwall Football Club's Occasional Licence, which
was required for the sale of beer on match days, was withdrawn. Millwall supporters' reputation for tough, yobbish
behaviour is obviously not new. But most people didn't
need the excuse of a football match to start downing enough
booze to set them off looking for a ruck.

In his work *Round London: Down East and Up West*, which
was originally published as a series of challenging articles,
the QC Montagu Williams expressed his particular fears
regarding the effect that alcohol was having on society, and
– again no surprise – specifically in the poorer districts:

It is now night, and we are in the neighbourhood of Brick Lane. Let us look at the public-houses hereabouts, and observe what is going on within and without their walls. They are frequented by the depraved, the dissolute, and the drunken. The male habitués are very bad, but the female habitués are even worse. Drunkard after drunkard staggers in at the doorway, and is freely supplied with drink. Outside, the scenes are revolting in the extreme. Men, in a ferocious stage of intoxication, quarrel, fight, and kick, and frenzied women fall upon one another, tearing out hair, scratching, spitting, and even inflicting wounds with their teeth. Verily this is a land flowing with beer and blood. These public-houses account for the long list of night charges that the magistrate has to deal with on Monday mornings at the Thames and Worship Street Police Courts. Whereas on ordinary mornings the number is about twenty or thirty, on Mondays it is from sixty to eighty. They are all of one description in so far as the offences arise from drink.

The introduction of the Beerhouse Act in 1830 probably hadn't helped curb excessive drinking among the poor. With the well-intentioned but ultimately misguided aim of diverting the labouring classes away from strong liquor – especially gin – the act allowed anyone to open a beer house or beer shop in exchange for the payment of a small fee. The beer houses could stay open – and here was the root of the problem – for twenty-four hours a day. It was admitted finally that these never-closing establishments – where the poor and even the homeless, if they could muster a few coppers, could have a warm, dry place to sit and drink – were capable of causing just as many problems as the gin palaces, if not more. And so the Public House Closing Act of 1864 was brought in. This required the premises to be closed between the hours of one and four in the morning. Not much of a change, but it was seen as an important step forward. By 1872, however, a full licensing act had been introduced that allowed for the option of closing on Sundays. But drink remained a curse for the people who took it to excess, especially those who didn't have the disposable income that was available to the better-off, who could afford to pay for their pleasures without having to go short in other areas of their lives. Even children were affected by the demon drink. Henry Mayhew put forward the very sensible, and what now seems obvious, argument that hiring and paying workers in public houses was hardly of help to those who couldn't control their intake, especially as they weren't being paid that much in the first place. He also pointed out that the wages being distributed in licensed premises would encourage illegal gambling and attract prostitutes willing and able to separate the inebriated men from what was left of their already meagre wages.

*

Drink was reported as causing more serious problems than separating fools from their money. In May 1874 the *Penny Illustrated Paper* reported a tragic crime in Bow Common:

The East-End Murders and suicide . . . directly illustrated the close connection between intemperance and crime . . . The fruitful source of immorality, the support of prostitution, the destroyer of home ties, and the most general incentive to murder, intemperance is the greatest curse of the kingdom . . . Not a week goes by without our having to chronicle some such domestic calamity . . . It was in a class of house occupied by artisans in Joseph-Street, Bow-Common, that John Blair murdered his wife and four children and then cut his own throat . . . As already quoted by us from The Times, 'The murderer and suicide was John Blair, a bricklayer . . . aged forty-nine, while his wife was thirty-four. The eldest child was Elizabeth, aged about thirteen, the next being Amelia, aged seven; the others were boys named William and Samuel, aged five years the one and four months the other; and the evidence disclosed that the father, who was probably mad from the effects of excess alcoholic drink, had mutilated the bodies of his little family in the most dreadful manner.' It came out at the inquest that . . . his brother-in-law said [that Blair] drank heavily at home . . . Elizabeth Cressy, a sharp little girl, living near the house in Joseph-street, Bow, said she used occasionally to fetch beer for the deceased man, and did so on the Friday afternoon before the tragedy took place.

The article goes on to describe the horrific mutilation of Blair's wife's and children's bodies.

It wasn't only men, of course, who could become killers after drinking. In the year following the Blair tragedy, the *Illustrated Police News* tells how an eighteen-year-old girl, Rebecca Carey, was charged with the murder of her own sister, Maria White, 'by fighting with her in a public house' in Bethnal Green, where the two of them had been drinking.

The sight of drunken women, whether murderous or not, was then, as now, deemed more deplorable than the sight of men in the same state. In the *East London Observer* on 19 September 1857 there was a piece about the 'amount of business' conducted in the Thames Police Court, Stepney. There seemed to be plenty going on, including one case which, according to the report, 'shocked' the magistrate:

> . . . *five prostitutes aged between 13 and 19 years old were charged with drunkenness and causing a disturbance in the public streets . . . [They were] 'walking the streets . . . decked out in tawdry finery, falls [a word first used in the early 1600s to describe a type of veil] and crinoline petticoats by procuresses and the infamous herd of brothel keepers, who infested every part of the district.'*

The girls probably claimed they were at least thirteen years of age as that had recently become the age of consent (having been raised from twelve).

The combination of drink and sex was a heady one for both the participants and the press, with the latter eager to report veiled but still titillating details, even in cases that resulted in no convictions. Take this item from October 1869, for example:

> *Mary Bennett and Ann Miller were charged on remand with stealing a purse, containing half a sovereign, two florins, and a shilling from*

the prosecutor . . . John Butler . . . the two prisoners came to him and asked him to treat them to some beer, and he did so. They afterwards followed him into Great St Helen's and behaved in a disgusting manner towards him, and then Miller took his purse and handed it to Bennett. The prosecutor denied that he was drunk. He said he was a married man and had a family . . . The purse was found on Bennett, but no money in it. One shilling in money was found on her, and a florin on Miller, but no half-sovereign. Mr Alderman Owden discharged the prisoners.

Just as alcohol was freely available everywhere, so too were drugs. Commercially, opium was mixed with alcohol to create a tincture, which made taking the drug more widely acceptable – as can be seen from the advertisement for Coca Wine at the beginning of the chapter. It also made for a cheaper way of getting intoxicated than buying straight drink.

When Walter Besant wrote about visiting an opium den close to the West India Dock, it wasn't the drug use that concerned him, but the din of what to his ears was the appalling Chinese music. He thought it sounded like 'a thousand fingernails scratching on the window, or ten thousand slate-pencils scratching on a schoolboy's slate'.

But if a 'genuine' exotic drug experience – smoking opium – was being sought, how easy was it for the punter to find? There has been a lot of discussion about whether a Chinese *demi-monde* of gambling, girls and drugs ever really existed near the docks of the East End. Critics of the idea have claimed that it was an invention based on sensationalized, fictional accounts from the likes of Charles Dickens, Sir Arthur Conan Doyle, Oscar Wilde and Max Rohmer. But from personal and family experience I can say that the original London Chinatown in Limehouse, while not huge, certainly existed. My father's Uncle Tom worked as a minder for a local, traditionally robed and plaited-haired Chinese 'businessman', known as Daddy Lee, who owned a gambling den specializing in *puk-apu*. As to what else went on in there, my father could only guess, but he said that there were strong hints that opium smoking was still taking place in the 1930s. In my early childhood we would buy Chinese food from Mr Ching, who had converted his little terraced house into a tiny restaurant, and there continues to be a Chinese community based in the area to this day, close to the old West India Dock near where I live, with social clubs, schools and a dragon sculpture celebrating its existence.

In contemporary Victorian accounts of visits to opium dens, there is no consensus as to the actual numbers of the establishments, which is not surprising considering their shady nature. The following two quotes describe dens around the Bluegate fields area, which was situated in Shadwell, close to the docks and warehouses, which would certainly have provided a source for smokable opium.

The first is taken from J. C. Parkinson's *Places and People, Being Studies from Life*:

Bluegate-fields is not in this police district, but the inspector will send a constable with me . . . There is no limit to the variety of nation-alities patronising the wretched hovel we are about to visit. From every quarter of the globe, and more immediately from every district in London, men come [here] the sole bond between them being a love of opium . . . Sailors, stewards, shop men, mountebanks, beggars, outcasts, and thieves meet on perfect equality in New-court, and there smoke themselves into dreamy stupefaction. There is a little colony of Orientals in the centre of Bluegate-fields, and in the centre of this colony is the opium divan. We reach it by a narrow passage leading up a narrow court, and easily gain admission on presenting ourselves at its door . . . The curious dry burning odour, which is making your eyelids quiver painfully, which is giving your temples the throbbing which so often predicates a severe headache, and which is tickling your gullet as if with a feather and fine dust, is from opium. Its fumes are curling overhead, the air is laden with them, and the bed-clothes and the rags hanging on the string above are all steeped through and through with the fascinating drug . . . As soon as we are sufficiently acclimatised to peer through the smoke, and after the bearded Oriental, who makes faces, and passes jibes at and for the company, has lighted a small candle in our honour, we see a sorry little apartment, which is almost filled by the French bedstead, on which half-a-dozen coloured men are coiled long-wise across its breadth, and in the centre of which is a common japan tray and opium lamp. Turn which way you will, you see or touch opium smokers. The cramped little chamber is one large opium pipe, and inhaling its atmosphere partially brings you under the drug's influence. Swarthy sombre faces loom out of dark corners, until the whole place seems alive with humanity; and turning to your guides you ask, with strange puzzlement, who Yahee's customers are, where they live, and how they obtain the wherewithal for the expensive luxury of opium-smoking . . . Mother Abdallah, who has just looked in from next door, interprets for us, and we exchange compliments and condolences . . . Mother Abdallah . . . who, from long association with Orientals, has mastered their habits and acquired their tongue. Cheeny (China) Emma and Lascar Sal, her neighbours, are both [away] from home this evening, but Mother Abdallah does the honours for her male friends with much grace and propriety – a pallid wrinkled woman of forty, who prepares and sells opium in another of the two-roomed hovels in the court: she confesses to smoking it too for company's sake, or if a friend asks her to, as you may say, and stoutly maintains the healthiness of the habit.

The second appears in our old friend James Greenwood's work *In Strange Company*:

Tiger Bay – or, more properly speaking, Blue Gate fields – has been so often described that it will be needless here to say more respecting it than that it is as tigerish as ever; that the dens to which, every night of the year, drunken sailors are betrayed, swarm and flourish openly and defiantly in spite of the police. I discovered that my friend, in describing the street that rejoiced in a Rehoboth Chapel and a Coal Whippers' Arms as 'not particularly inviting,' had done it no injustice. It is in the very heart of the Bay, and from end to end it presents an unbroken scene of vice and depravity of the most hideous sort. Almost every house is one of 'ill fame' . . . There was no one at home but the opium-master's wife; but as she is English, I experienced no difficulty in making known to her my desire. She exhibited not the least amazement that one of her own countrymen should have a craving after the celestial luxury . . . She was very ill, poor woman. It was killing her, she said, this constant breathing of the fumes of the subtle drug her husband dealt in. She didn't mind it, she had grown used to it, but it 'told on her,' and lodged in her chest, and gave her a cough.

'You mean that it is the smoke from your customers' pipes that affects you,' I remarked.

'There is no smoke from the pipes, it's too precious for that,' replied the woman. 'Nobody ought to smoke opium . . . who is as wasteful as that,' And she accompanied the severe observation with a shake of her head, and a glance that betokened her fathomless pity for a person in my benighted condition.

'Then how do the fumes, or the smoke, or whatever it is, get into your throat, ma'am?' I enquired, humbly.

'It's the preparing of it chiefly,' said she, 'which I'd better be doing now, if you have no objection.'

On the contrary, I was but too grateful for the opportunity of witnessing such a mystery. I was presently amazed, too, as well as thankful; for, dropping on her hands and knees, she crawled a little way under the bedstead, and again emerged with a saucepan — a common iron saucepan, capable of holding perhaps two quarts. This was a painful stab at my reverence for opium. Had I seen a vessel of ancient porcelain, or even a brazen pipkin, it would not have been so shocking; but a vulgar, smutty pot, such as potatoes are boiled in! I began to have doubts lest, after all, I had come to the wrong

*shop; but a searching question soon drew out clear evidence that I
had been preceded in my visit by the illustrious travellers of whom
I had heard.*

Among other descriptions of dens operating in the neighbourhood is one from Charles Dickens Junior's *Dictionary
of London*. He didn't think much of the establishments but,
astonishingly, could still contend that they were enough of
a popular draw to be visited by the whole spectrum of
society – including royalty.

*The best known of these justly-named 'dens' is that of one Johnstone,
who lives in a garret off Ratcliff-high way, and for a consideration
allows visitors to smoke a pipe which has been used by many crowned
heads in common with poor Chinese sailors who seek their native
pleasure in Johnstone's garret . . . A similar establishment of a
slightly superior – or it might be more correct to say a shade less
nauseating – class is that of Johnny Chang, at the London and St
Katharine Coffee-house, in the Highway itself.*

While reports of opium smoking only describe the activity
as happening in dubious areas like those surrounding the
docks, the drug might well have been smoked in private,
more luxurious premises, because opiates, what we would
today regard as class-A drugs, were widely available in other
forms for legal – and respectable – purchase across the
counter, which was openly done by the likes of Jane Carlyle
and Wilkie Collins.

But its use wasn't confined to 'celebrities'. In a coroner's inquiry held at the Grasshopper Tavern in Whitechapel following the death of 66-year-old Henry Davis, it was recorded that he was a habitual user of opium, having believed that it was good for his chest and heart. Unfortunately, what was described as an 'excessive quantity' of the substance 'stopped it'.

The following item from the periodical *Chemist and Druggist* of January 1863 is notable for the fact that the dubious manner of acquiring the substance rather than its nature – or quantity – is what seems to worry the writer:

The plaintiff is a wholesale chemist and druggist at Bishopsgate Street Within, and bought some parcels of opium, varying from 35 lb. to 45 lb., from a person named Dudley, who is since dead. He had also purchased a parcel of 23 ½ lb. from a person named Crane, a dealer in drugs, in 1861. Both these parcels had been put into boxes and forwarded to Mr Lindo for sale . . . On the 19th July, Whicher, the detective . . . called on the plaintiff, and interrogated him as to where and from whom he obtained the last parcel. The plaintiff . . . refused to tell. The officers took him to the office of the London Docks, where questions were put to him, but he still refused to give any information. The plaintiff commenced an action against Mr Lindo to recover the cases of opium . . . A ship called the Brenda *had brought over a valuable cargo of 101 chests of opium, and according to the statement of Mr Brooks, an opium broker . . . the cargo of the* Brenda *was the best of the kind that had been exported to this country for years . . . The defendants had been robbed of a part of the Brenda's cargo, and it was contended that the opium in dispute formed a part of the stolen property . . . The jury intimated that they entertained a very strong opinion in favour of the defendants . . . A verdict was entered for [them].*

Mothers used opium-based remedies from laudanum to Dover's Powders to quieten their babies, which sometimes led to tragic results, but with even the revered Mrs Beeton advising its use in the chapter of her 1861 *Book of Household Management* entitled 'The Rearing, Management and Diseases of Infancy and Childhood', it is hardly surprising that distraught women jumped at the opportunity of 'soothing' their children. As will be seen later, baby farmers were particularly good customers for the calming tinctures.

But the unfaithful potency of laudanum was widely understood, as this 1874 item from the *Penny Illustrated Paper* shows:

At Clerkenwell Police Court . . . Elizabeth Burroughes, aged twenty-one, a well-dressed, lady-like young woman, described on the charge-sheet as a dressmaker . . . was charged before Mr Barstow with attempting to destroy herself by taking a quantity of laudanum at Phoenix-street, Somerstown. When she had partly recovered she informed Inspector Calder that she had no relations in London, and only a brother in India . . . until lately she carried on a business at Wheatley Oxfordshire, but that business she had sold and had come to London to look after her young man. The previous night she had fallen in with him, but he had treated her coldly and with disdain, and then she felt that she was tired of life. The defendant, who appeared very ill and depressed in spirits, said that she exceedingly regretted what she had done. Sad were her thoughts when she had taken the poison and felt that it was taking effect, and she was very thankful to the police and to them for the care they had taken of her.

Mr Barstow wasn't as sympathetic as the police. He pointed out to poor young Elizabeth the enormity and cowardliness of her actions, then found her guilty and remanded her to the House of Detention while further enquiries were made.

An advertisement for Geraudel's Pastilles, which cured 'coughs, colds, catarrh, influenza, asthma, throat irritation, loss of voice and all kindred troubles', proudly boasted that no opium or other narcotic drugs were used in their manufacture. And as can be seen in this 1892 report from the *Penny Illustrated Paper*, doctors were becoming disturbed about the increasing abuse of drugs:

During the Congress on Hygiene recently held in London, some of the most distinguished physicians and scientists were discussing the terrible ravages of morphinomania spreading amongst all sorts and conditions of men and women in England, France, and the United States of North America. Once the habit of taking morphia or opium is acquired, and it is acquired with incredible rapidity, there is no way to check the morphinomaniacs indulgent weakness for the poisonous drug, and, of course, no end to the disorders arising and developing in his or her constitution, until death comes swift and sure to strike the emaciated body, or, worse than all, a horrible madness overcomes the brain. Volumes over volumes have been written on the dread consequences of taking morphia and opium in whatever form or guise. Newspapers and medical periodicals never cease to warn the public [about] the subtle yet fatal danger of yielding to a habit which, though not so repulsive and visibly abominable as alcoholic inebriation, is yet a hundredfold more noxious.

The article went on to condemn the casual use of opiate-laced remedies, but not everyone was a willing or even knowing participant in the Victorian drug culture that so worried the congress. The incident described below from *The Times* of 7 September 1877 is unpleasantly reminiscent of modern-day reports about the devious and unlawful use of so-called 'date rape' drugs such as Rohypnol, GHB and ketamine:

Dulwich has recently been the scene of a criminal outrage, which has created the utmost indignation and has had the most deplorable results. The victims were two young ladies, the daughters of highly respectable parents, residing in Brixton, and one of them has since died, while the other lies in a critical state . . . it appears that the two young ladies while walking one evening down the Brixton-road were accosted by two well-dressed, gentlemanly-looking men, and importuned to accompany them to a theatre in the Strand. This request the girls refused to comply with, whereupon they were asked as an alternative to go for a walk. To this request they unluckily yielded. Accordingly the four strolled as far as Dulwich, and on arriving there the girls were asked to partake of refreshment. They accordingly entered a public house, and it is believed that here the drink of which they partook was drugged by one of the men. Soon after swallowing it the girls became stupefied, and while in that condition the scoundrels succeeded in outraging them. Then, unseen by the landlady, the two men shortly after quitted the place together. Not suspecting what had happened, and being, of course, ignorant of the respectability of the poor girls, the landlady treated them as persons of questionable repute, and at about 11 o'clock at night ejected them from her house. Frenzied, as the parents say, and overwhelmed with a sense of disgrace, they had not the courage, nor had they probably the sense, to retrace their steps home. The poor creatures, therefore, wandered about all night in a distracted state and did not return home even the next day. Meanwhile the parents instituted inquiries in all directions, and at the expiration of two days the girls were found in a most deplorable state huddled together in one of the recesses on Blackfriars-bridge. Even then they did not seem to have recovered entire consciousness, but told the story to their parents as best they could. One of the poor girls did not long survive her shame. A few days after her return home she expired, it is said from the effects of the administered drug, and the other has ever since been in such a state of prostration that her life is despaired of, and in the opinion of her medical attendants her mind is likely in any case to be affected. It is to be hoped that the authors of this most shocking and heartless crime will soon be in the hands of the police.

The pity is that the men involved in the attack could easily have found females who would have been available to them – in every sense – at a far lower cost to all concerned.

4

THE SEX TRADE, PORN, VICE AND BABY FARMERS

When all is said and done, it [prostitution] is, and I believe ever will be, ineradicable.

William Acton, *Prostitution*, 1870

I dare not follow our author any further in his description of the personal beauties of Starlight Sal. Were I to do so, it would be the fate of this book to be flung in to the fire, and every decent man who met me would regard himself justified in kicking or cursing me . . . and yet tons of this bird-lime of the pit [pornography] is vended in London every day of the Christian year.

James Greenwood, *The Seven Curses of London*, 1869

It is a veritable slave trade that is going on around us; but as it takes place in the heart of London, it is a scandal – an outrage on public morality – even to allude to it.

W. T. Stead, *Pall Mall Gazette*, 6 July 1885

*

Henry Mayhew shocked the sensitivities of his readers when he wrote about the lives of the women who worked as seamstresses. They were so poorly paid when they could find employment, and were so unsure about whether work would be available again when they couldn't, that they had to resort to supplementing their incomes by prostituting themselves. Even if Mayhew was using his undoubted skills as a journalist and was purely seeking to shock – such was the vogue for sensational reporting – he still did a valuable job in exposing the realities of those women's lives. Other social investigators of the period supported his claims, and it was plain that while some high-end prostitutes had a choice about whether or not they entered the sex trade, and did well, financially at least, out of their chosen profession, there were those who had no such choice or reward.

Andrew Mearns in particular went to great lengths to show how trying to earn an honest living could be almost impossible for the poorest and least-educated classes, and not just because of the shockingly low rates of pay they were offered, but also because of the corrupting influences which surrounded them:

Incest is common and no form of vice and sensuality causes surprise or attracts attention . . . The vilest practices are looked upon with the most matter-of-fact indifference. The low parts of London are the sink into which the filthy and abominable from all parts of the country seem to flow. Entire courts are filled with thieves, prostitutes and liberated convicts. In one street are 35 houses, 32 of which are known to be brothels . . . numbers of women and children, some of the latter only seven years old, are employed in sack making, for which they get a farthing each. In one house was found a widow and her half-idiot daughter making palliasses [covers for straw mattresses] at 1 ¾ d. each. Here is a woman who has a sick husband and a little child to look after. She is employed at shirt finishing at 3d. a dozen, and by the utmost effort can only earn 6d. a day, out of which she has to find her own thread. Another, with a crippled hand, maintains herself and a blind husband by match-box making, for which she is remunerated 2 ¼ d. a gross [out of which] she has to pay a girl a penny a gross to help her. Others obtain at Covent Garden in the season 1d. or 2d. a peck for shelling peas, or 6d. a basket for walnuts . . . they do well if their labour brings them 10d. or a shilling a day.

It was women such as these who, when desperation finally took over, would have little alternative but to trade on their raw wits and their bodies – a stark choice between street prostitution and the shame and deprivations of the workhouse.

They had every reason to resist going into the bastilles, those hated places. In there the harsh parish regime of the

Board of Guardians would see that they were separated from husbands and children. Coarse uniforms had to be worn, the food was gruel and bread, and the work was hard and monotonous. The system was designed to be harsh, the intention being to deter the malingerer. But it could go too far. There was a report in the medical press in 1838 of child inmates of the workhouse being system-atically starved, flogged and held in the stocks for days on end; and there was a notorious case in the 1840s when starving inmates attacked one another over the fragments of decayed meat left on the bones that they had been charged to pound to dust for use as fertilizer.

At least if the women chose street prostitution rather than going into the spike there was the hope that things *might* get better, and that they could then return to paid employment of a potentially less dangerous and degrading kind than walking the streets and having sex with strangers.

When writing about the casinos – the popular 'dance halls' – favoured by men seeking the company of women, William Acton stated categorically that the women there were 'of course all prostitutes' of a very low sort, though he judged that they were a step up from the 'street girls'. The places themselves sound rather glamorous in a louche, gin-palace kind of a way:

> *The principal dancing rooms of London are the two casinos known respectively as the Argyll Rooms and the Holborn. Formerly there was a striking difference between these two places, the one receiving*

the upper, the other the under, current of the fast life of London; now, however, there is little of this distinction noticeable, and the visitor in quest, not of amusement, but of information, may feel assured that a visit to one is for all practical purposes a visit to both. They are open for music and dancing every evening, except Sunday, from half-past eight o'clock to twelve. The visitor, on passing the doors, finds himself in a spacious room, the fittings of which are of the most costly description, while brilliant gas illuminations, reflected by numerous mirrors, impart a fairy-like aspect to the scene. The company is, of course, mixed. Many of the men resorting to such places seek no doubt the opportunity of indulging their vicious propensities . . .

Acton was well aware of how highly the women valued the casinos for the opportunity they offered to earn reasonable money:

The proprietor, indeed, is careful to maintain the appearance, at least, of decorum among his visitors. Should any woman misconduct herself, she is pointed out to the door-keepers, with instructions not to admit her again to the rooms. No punishment could be heavier, no sentence more rigorously carried out. She will attempt in vain by disguise to avoid recognition, or by bribes to soften the watchful janitor. Her efforts will be met with some such rebuke as this: 'It's no use trying it on, Miss Polly; the gov'nor says you are not to go in, and, of course, you can't!' Her only chance of obtaining remission of the sentence is to induce some friend to plead with the proprietor on her behalf, who may, but does not always, readmit her after an exile of three months, and on her promising to behave herself in the strictest manner for the future. On the whole, judging of the women who frequent these rooms by their dress, deportment, and general appearance, the visitor might be inclined to suppose them to belong to the kept mistress rather than the prostitute class. This is, however, not the case, as, with a few exceptions, they fall within the latter denomination. Many of them, no doubt, have a friend who visits them regularly, and who makes them a fixed allowance, not sufficient to keep them altogether, but substantial enough to make them careful in selecting their customers, and careful about accepting the company of a man in any way objectionable. This arrangement is perfectly understood by the 'friend' who pays his periodical visits, and to whom, of course, the woman is always at home.

He went on to describe how, at midnight, when the casinos closed, other places were sought out by the men with a mission to find sex for sale, places such as the Haymarket – then a very dubious area, despite repeated attempts to clean it up:

Observe the stale, drooping lobsters, the gaping oysters, the mummified cold fowl with trappings of flabby parsley, and the pale fly-spotted cigars; and then look in the chemists windows, and see by the open display in which direction his chief trade tends. Study the character of the doubtful people you see standing in the doorways – always waiting for somebody as doubtful as themselves – and wonder what the next plan is to be . . . It is always an offensive place to pass, even in the daytime, but at night it is absolutely hideous . . .

Acton was to venture further east to continue his investigations into the lives of prostitutes, studying the problems there under the protection and watchful eye of the police. Unfortunately, he wasn't helped by the weather, the women having been driven indoors, but the local officers proved to be a useful source of information:

Some shades of prostitution unknown to the more fashionable West are to be discerned in the East End of London. To acquaint myself with these, I made a pilgrimage in company with Captain Harris, Assistant Commissioner of Police, to the notorious Ratcliffe Highway. We were attended by the Superintendent of the Executive Branch of the Metropolitan police, and two Inspectors. The night being very wet, the streets were comparatively empty, and therefore I can say little or nothing from personal observation about the condition of street prostitution in this district. [But] I understand that it in no respect differs from what we see elsewhere. The first house we entered was one in which prostitutes reside. It was kept by a dark, swarthy, crisp-haired Jewess, half creole in appearance, who stated that she was a widow, and that having married a Christian, she had been discarded by her own people. To my inquiry whether she knew of many Jewesses who led a life of prostitution, she replied in the negative, giving as a reason that the Jews look after their people better than Christians, and assist them when in distress. The police Inspectors corroborated her statement, which seems to contradict the prevalent notion that houses of ill-fame are frequently kept by Jewesses. We went upstairs, and saw the rooms, eight in number, which were let out to as many women. The landlady told us that they pay 2s when they bring home a visitor, and she thought that on an average they are lucky when they bring two each in the course of the evening. This woman was clearly indisposed to let us into her secrets, seeing us accompanied by the Inspectors . . . The utmost pressure put upon them is, perhaps, that they are induced to go out and persevere in prostitution when otherwise indisposed to do so. When ill, they apply to the hospital, and St Bartholomew's appeared to be the favourite establishment. This house may be taken as a fair sample of the brothels existing in the East End of London.

As with the opium dens, the numbers of brothels were not easily calculated, due to their very nature. Donald Rumbelow, in his *Complete Jack the Ripper*, quotes figures from the *Lancet* which suggest that in the East End in 1857 one house in sixty was a brothel and one in sixteen women worked as a prostitute. Despite the respected nature of the journal, the figures seem remarkably high, but not all of the women would have been full-time prostitutes and not all the places they worked from would have been formal brothels. There is, however, plenty of evidence for the existence of many such establishments, along with descriptions of the various specialist tastes for which they catered. They ranged from the poorest case houses of Spitalfields and Whitechapel – these were to become notorious in the autumn of 1888, when 'Jack' went on his killing spree – to the expensive establishments run by the likes of Mary Jeffries, a woman noted for her provision of young girls and of flagellation chambers for the benefit of her wealthy clients. There was also a whole range of types of people who worked in the brothels, not to mention a vast difference between those who were made to be part of the sex trade by means of physical force, blackmail, bullying or desperation, and the consenting adults who opted to earn money in that way. But while coercion can never be acceptable, can choosing prostitution as a way of life ever be? It was this dilemma that had Victorian moralists getting their metaphorical knickers in a twist over the likes of Catherine Walters – one of the women who worked at the top end of the market.

Catherine, born in Liverpool in the late 1830s, would eventually become internationally known as a courtesan under the pet name of Skittles. She came to London in the 1850s with the direct intention of cashing in on her great beauty. A considerable horsewoman and well aware of her effect on men, she had especially tight-fitting riding habits made and would parade around Hyde Park, leaving gawping observers wondering, as she rode past, whether she could possibly be wearing any underwear beneath such figure-hugging clothes.

Catherine quickly became the Victorian equivalent of a superstar celebrity today, attracting the attention of rich and powerful men who sought out her 'company', and she had one particularly scandalous relationship with Lord Hartington, heir to the Duke of Devonshire. When high-minded disgust condemning the unsuitable liaison appeared in the newspapers, which displayed the same prurience shown by certain sections of today's press when revealing similar scandals, the relationship was ended. But it wasn't the end of Skittles's career, and she continued to work and prosper.

There were other prostitutes who became famous, including Victorian household names such as Agnes Willoughby, Kate Cook and Annie King, who was better known as Mabel Grey. As Mabel, she became one of the most photographed women of the whole century. But such glamour was not the norm in the sex trade, not even when it appeared that the exchanges were consensual.

The case of *Garner* vs. *Woods*, for instance, which was heard at Lambeth County Court, was brought over an unpaid debt and it shows a very different side to sex for sale. The plaintiff had been 'lending his wife' out to another man for nine shillings a week, and he was putting in a claim for £5 8s 6d, this being

> *twelve weeks' allowance . . . in consideration [of] allowing his wife to cohabit peaceably with the defendant. Upon the plaintiff stepping into the witness-box and stating the grounds for the action, the learned judge, in a most indignant tone, told him to stand down [and that the court] could not take cognisance of so shameful a claim . . .*

The reality for most prostitutes in Victorian London was hanging around the pubs and the common lodging houses at the Flower and Dean Street end of Brick Lane. These cheapest of the lodging houses, where individuals paid a few pence for a coffin-like bed and the use of a filthy, smoke-filled communal 'kitchen' housed in the basement, were little more than thieves' dens. They were places where the hopeless, the desperate and the dangerous rubbed ill-fated shoulders, all leeching off or corrupting each other, running whores, fencing goods and generally lying low from the forces of the law.

The experience of the women who plied their trade from there was far more like that of the dead-eyed smackheads who are still slouching around today in the same haunts as those women who became the victims of Jack the Ripper. They have far more to do with the reality of that world than the fairy-tale whirl of sparkling teeth, glossy hair and designer clothes supposedly experienced by cheap-end prostitutes like the one portrayed by Julia Roberts in the film *Pretty Woman* as her life is transformed and she shops with her handsome and adoring client's credit cards.

Also working at the bottom end of the market were the 'dress lodgers', the prostitutes who didn't even have the wherewithal to clothe themselves for carrying out their business and so lived in or frequented the dress houses. The ones who 'lived in', as it were, are described here by William Acton:

> *They were maintained . . . by persons who furnished board, lodging, and clothes to a number of prostitutes whom they sent out into the streets under guard of servants, or kept at home to receive visitors. The girls, who, it is needless to say, were of the most utterly degraded class, received but a small share of the wages of their sin . . . The*

rouged and whitewashed creatures, with painted lips and eyebrows, and false hair . . . were watched by persons of their own sex, employed purposely to prevent their abstraction of the lodging-house finery, and [to prevent] clandestine traffic with men. These wretched women, virtually slaves . . . live with their landlady, by whom they are provided with food, dress, and lodging, all which are charged to the women at an exorbitant price, and the landlady usually contrives to keep them in her debt . . .

But they weren't all what Acton described as 'wretched women' – some of them were far too young to be described in that way. The legal age of consent for girls was twelve years old up until 1875, when it was raised to thirteen. While not a huge improvement, this at least went some way to protecting children – technically at least, although youngsters didn't always know their birth dates and so could claim to be any age within reason. This was not unusual for poorer people in Victorian times; my father's mother, for instance, who was born in Ireland in the late 1880s, had no idea when she was born, but would celebrate her birthday twice a year, on St Patrick's Day and Pancake Day.

The age of consent was changed partly as a result of pressure from campaigners, including Josephine Butler, the great crusader for, among other things, the revoking of the Contagious Diseases Acts. These acts had sanctioned the enforced imprisonment and intimate medical examination of prostitutes suspected of passing syphilis on to soldiers and sailors, among whom the disease had become rife. Without treatment of the men, the efforts were pointless, not that the available medication was of much use, ranging as it did from highly dangerous application of mercury to totally useless quack potions, pills and lotions.

Josephine Butler was also noted for the part she played in the campaign to end what had become known as white slavery. It was widely acknowledged that overcrowding led to cases of incest in the slums, with young girls being at particular risk, but it was the selling of virgin girls – in this case to foreign brothels, much as Eastern European girls are being illegally trafficked today – with which Butler was concerned. Determined to expose the trade, she went to the journalist William Stead, who was the editor of the *Pall Mall Gazette*, and to Bramwell Booth of the Salvation Army to help her bring it to the attention of the British public. In 1885 Stead did a spectacular job of doing just that, with a scandalous stunt and a series of articles that became known collectively as the *Maiden Tribute to Modern Babylon*. Unfortunately, the well-intentioned exercise was to backfire, with Stead being sent to prison, and despite the publicity and Butlers efforts, the buying and selling of young girls continued.

The articles provided an account of how Stead was able to purchase a young girl, Eliza Armstrong, from her mother with the help of a one-time prostitute for five pounds. After the child was chloroformed and verified *virgo intacta* by a midwife, she was transported abroad – actually being taken to Paris by a female member of the Salvation Army – and so the deed was proved possible. Stead's pieces were preaching while also being titillating and were big sellers. But his undoing would be his accusation that there were brothels which were frequented by the rich and famous, some of whom he stated were being protected from police prosecution simply for those reasons, while the rest were protected because of the cash payments they made directly to the force. The official reason for Stead being imprisoned was his open 'purchase' of the thirteen-year-old girl.

The *Pall Mall Gazette* of n November 1885 quoted several press reports on Stead's trial, including this one from the *Daily Chronicle*:

> *We cannot and we do not refuse to credit Mr Stead with the best of motives. He may be an enthusiast or a fanatic, but his enthusiasm or fanaticism was roused by the contemplation of the worst of crimes; and though it was directed into illegal channels it sought to accomplish a great good in the interest of society. We may hope that as the law has been thus vindicated it may be found practicable to temper justice with mercy.*

Before being scandalized by the treatment of poor Victorian children and the ability of the rich and powerful to protect themselves from prosecution, we should look to behaviour in our own age. In a recent BBC television programme, aired after the Gary Glitter child abuse trial, two journalists went to Cambodia, posing as Western sex tourists, so they could investigate child prostitution. They were offered 'unopened' girls of thirteen years old.

It could be argued that just as the so-called Satanic abuse cases of the 1980s were responsible for deflecting attention away from the real problem – the failure to deal in any significant way with the existence of child abuse and neglect in all its forms – so the sensational stories of girls being held and sold against their will might well have deflected attention from the real problem in the nineteenth century: why so many girls – and boys – were being driven into the Victorian sex trade in the first place. But Stead had proved his point that a virgin child could be bought and abducted, and even if his displeasing the establishment did see him prosecuted, his actions resulted in the introduction of the Criminal Law Amendment Act, which saw the age of consent being raised from thirteen to sixteen. Unfortunately, a further amendment was added to the law as it made its passage through Parliament which introduced the criminalization of all homosexual acts – even in private – labelling them 'acts of gross indecency'. It was this section of the law that was to result in a case, once again involving members of the establishment, that became known as the Cleveland Street Scandal – as much a scandal because of those involved as for the apparent conspiracy which protected them.

The story began in July 1889, when a young telegraph boy came under police suspicion for possible robbery from his workplace because of the unusually large amount of money he was carrying. When he protested that he wasn't a thief but had been given the money by the wealthy gentlemen who visited Charles Hammond's house in Cleveland Street to buy sex, the investigation into the male brothel began. It wasn't to be a straightforward process. When Chief Inspector Abberline – who had become famous for his part in the Jack the Ripper investigations of the previous year – turned up at the house, there was no sign of Hammond or any of the 'gentlemen' visitors. There was a person, however, for the police to interview: one of the telegraph lads by the name of Newlove, who was also implicated in procurement of boys as prostitutes. He decided to cooperate and was not shy about naming the men who frequented the brothel. There was an embarrassing number of aristocrats on his list, including the Earl of Euston, Lord Arthur Somerset and even, so it was rumoured, Prince Albert Victor – known as Eddy – son of the Prince of Wales and a man pointed to by many a supposedly well-informed finger as being none other than Jack the Ripper. Adding to this heady brew was the allegation that there existed a ring of powerful homosexuals who, linked through Freemasonry, were involved in the whole unpleasant and illegal business.

It was due to an unexplained delay in sending the police chief inspector to raid the Cleveland Street address that the only arrests were those of Newlove and a couple of young men who worked in the brothel, and also Lord Somerset's solicitor, who was later found guilty of attempting to pervert the course of justice. No one else could be traced. The leniency of the subsequent sentencing – in contradiction to that stipulated by the Criminal Law Amendment Act – added to the growing belief that there was a conspiracy to protect those involved and that time had been allowed for them to escape. There was one man with connections to the scandal, however, who did receive something like a full sentence. This was Ernest Parke.

Parke was the editor of the *North London Press* and he dared to name both Euston and Somerset. He then made the further mistake of printing his view that they had been allowed to flee England, with a further accusation that it was because they knew the identity of somebody involved who was even higher up the social scale – strongly implying a royal connection. Euston sued, and when Parke failed to prove his case he was found guilty of libel and jailed for a year.

Some thirty-five years earlier another notorious episode had been reported in *The Times* during July and August 1854. The articles contain the rather curious note that the police officer admitted that he had been witnessing the incidents that led to the case being brought over a period of eighteen months, but for some unexplained reason had made no effort to put a stop to them during that time.

John Challis, an old man about 60 years of age, dressed in the pastoral garb of a shepherdess of the golden age, and George Campbell, aged 35, who described himself as a lawyer, and appeared completely equipped in female attire of the present day, were placed at the bar before Sir R.W. Carden charged with being found disguised as women in the Druids'-hall, in Turnagain-lane, an unlicensed dancing-room, for the purpose of exciting others to commit an unnatural offence.

Inspector Teague said – From information I received relative to the frequent congregation of certain persons for immoral practices at the Druids'-hall, I proceeded thither in company with Sergeant Goodeve at about 2 o'clock this morning. I saw a great many persons dancing there, and among the number were the prisoners, who rendered themselves very conspicuous by their disgusting and filthy conduct. I suspected that the prisoners and several others who were present in female attire were of the male sex, and I left the room for the purpose of obtaining further assistance, so as to secure the whole of the parties, but when we got outside Campbell came out after us, and, taking us by the arms, was about to speak, when I exclaimed, 'That is a man,' upon which he turned round and ran back immediately to the Druids'-hall. I returned and took Campbell into custody and observing Challis, whom I have frequently seen there before, behaving with two men as if he were a common prostitute, I took charge of him also . . .

The final day of the trial was reported in *The Times* as follows, and in view of the shameful tradition of greater lenience being shown towards people of a certain class by their peers, there is a perhaps unsurprising conclusion:

Sir R.W. Carden – I was informed . . . that your object in visiting Druids'-hall was to see vice in all its enormity, in order that you might correct it from the pulpit, and . . . that was the excuse you made for going to such places.

Campbell — . . . I certainly did wish to see a little of London life without mixing with its abominations.

Sir R. W. Carden — And you thought that dressing yourself in women's attire was the best way of avoiding those abominations? I must say it was a very imprudent course . . . I certainly hope you now see the folly of indulging in such extraordinary freaks, as you term them, and that you deeply feel how degrading it is to a man of education . . . to be placed in such a position . . . However, under the circumstances, I am willing to believe it was nothing more than an act of the grossest folly, and that you now sincerely repent your imprudent conduct.

A similarly lenient result followed the trial of Frederick Park and Ernest Boulton, despite the latter appearing in the dock in a cherry-coloured silk evening dress, bare-armed save for bracelets and with a wig done up in a chignon; his companion was sporting a dress of fetching dark green satin. The pair were known for appearing in public in female attire and full make-up, frequenting the theatre and social events, and strolling through the Burlington Arcade, winking and making little noises in order to attract men. As cross-dressing was a minor offence, there were efforts to prove that sodomy had taken place, and an examination by a police surgeon was carried out. In spite of his positive evidence that it had, and the production of packs of incriminating letters between the two and the other men being tried with them, the case collapsed and all of the defendants were acquitted.

A more robust view towards such behaviour was held by members of the Society for the Suppression of Vice. The following appeared in January 1872 in the *Leisure Hour*, *a* very popular 2d weekly aimed at a family readership:

This society . . . has laboured unremittingly to check the spread of open vice and immorality, and more especially to preserve the minds of the young from contamination by exposure to the corrupting influence of impure and licentious books, prints, and other publications; its difficulties have been greatly increased by the application of photography, multiplying, at an insignificant cost, filthy representations from living models, and the improvement in the postal service has further introduced facilities for secret trading which were previously unknown. There is but too great reason to know that in spite of all efforts these polluting productions are still circulated throughout the country, principally through the post-office . . . but for [the Society's] existence, the trade in licentious publications would be carried on with impunity . . . This society has been the means of suppressing the circulation of several low and vicious periodicals . . . within a few years it has seized and destroyed the following enormous mass of corrupting matters: 140,213 obscene prints, pictures, and photographs; 21,772 books and pamphlets; five tons of letterpress in sheets, besides large quantities of infidel and blasphemous publications; 17,060 sheets of obscene songs, catalogues, circulars, and handbills; 5,712 cards, snuff-boxes, and vile articles; 844 engraved copper and steel plates; 480 lithographic stones; 146 wood blocks; 11 printing presses, with type and apparatus; 81 cwt. of type, including the stereotype of several works of the vilest description.

But despite the impressive efforts of the society, vice thrived, with the trade in pornography continuing to do particularly well. Drury Lane and Holywell Street – close to the Strand, where the Aldwych is now situated – had become the base for the publishers and sellers of pornography, many of whom, such as William Dugdale, made impressive profits. One of the big sellers was a fictional 'autobiography' telling the story of the supposed life and times of Jack Saul, a celebrity male prostitute, which described in great detail how a man could make a handsome living plying his trade in that supposedly prim and proper era. In the shops around Holywell Street the pornographic literature was being sold alongside pictures, photographs, brothel listings and directories suggesting gay pick-up venues, which were all popular sellers.

Just as the widespread access to computer technology has seen an explosion in prosecutions related to the dissemination and downloading of illegal images from the Internet, so the Society for the Suppression of Vice, which had been set up at the beginning of the century, found their work ever more demanding as new photographic techniques were developed and then exploited by the pornographers. This was happening alongside the spread of the railway network and the subsequent improvements to the countrywide postal system, which meant that pornographic material could be sent discreetly to clients either too shy or too distant from the shops to make regular personal visits. And even back in Victoria's time it wasn't only still images that were being circulated. In 1896 Esme Collings, one of Britain's earliest film-makers was running a studio in Brighton. It was there that he made a short film called *Woman Undressing*, widely acknowledged to be the world's first pornographic movie.

But in the spirit of the actual meaning of the word, pornography was still most prolific in its written form, encompassing everything from cheap booklets produced in those streets off the Strand for the less well-heeled enthusiast to the massive collection put together by Henry Ashbee. On his death this would be donated to the British Museum, where it was held in the library under the terms of restricted access – thus keeping it from the gaze of the 'wrong sort' of person.

Ashbee serves as a great example of one of the dualities of Victorian life – the respectable and the reprobate all rolled up into one. A successful businessman, married with four children, and with a passionate, scholarly interest in Spanish literature, he was also an obsessive collector of porn with a particular interest in flagellation. His learned approach served him well in both areas of his life. He amassed an extensive library of Spanish texts, specializing in the works of Cervantes, while also being the meticulous compiler of three privately printed bibliographies of pornography, and a directory of specialist brothels where flagellation could be indulged in, which also listed their specific areas of expertise. He certainly appeared to know his stuff, and may yet have an even greater claim to fame than his collections. A 2001 book by Ian Gibson, *The*

Erotomaniac, argues convincingly – against previous claims to the contrary – that Ashbee was probably the author of the notoriously obscene 'diaries' *My Secret Life*, written under the name of 'Walter', which gave an exhaustively comprehensive account of the protagonist's sexual tastes and supposed experiences.

So the sex and porn trades were doing well, but regardless of moral judgement or ethical opprobrium, and the risk of contracting STDs, there was an additional problem for even 'good' Victorian women engaging in sexual activity – the risk of pregnancy. The lack of reliable, affordable contraception, no safe abortion and no decent welfare services to speak of meant that pregnancy was always a risk and could at times prove to be a disaster. This was particularly true for the unmarried or those with an existing brood of children, and desperate women would be driven to pay the baby farmers who advertised their services in the press as carers of children.

In theory, the idea was that the farmers were kind fosterers who would mind the little ones, committed to their care on a temporary basis, or that they would adopt them permanently, or, if this wasn't possible, that they would make every Christian effort to find decent families to do so. But in practice this was often no more than a charade and the children were in fact abandoned to a cruel fate.

Some did find new homes – not always exactly decent or the most suitable, when they were being sold into the clutches of sham beggars as props for scamming the public

– but there were more tragic stories of neglect, abuse and even murder.

Moved to scrutinize the practice of baby-farming, James Greenwood concluded:

We are lamentably ignorant both of the gigantic extent and the pernicious working of this mischief It is only when some loud-crying abuse of the precious system makes itself heard in our criminal courts, and is echoed in the newspapers, or when some adventurous magazine writer in valiant pursuit of his avocation, directs his inquisitive nose in the direction indicated that the public at large hear anything either of the farmer or the farmed.

He bemoaned the fact that the public was shocked and appalled by such stories but then merely moved on to the next sensation brought to its attention by the press. He later went on to say that 'This is the unhappy fate that attends nearly all our social grievances.' And, as he pointed out, it is between the cracks of public outrage that injustice slips.

Greenwood related the story of Caroline Savill of Bow, who, it was revealed in court, had seen five of the eleven children in her care die – that is to say, five of the eleven who were known about at the time of the prosecution. Numbers and the identity of others in her 'care' were neither investigated nor followed up. The children farmed out to Savill were reported as being found in filthy, makeshift cots made from egg boxes with nothing but straw for bedding;

they had broken limbs and had finally met their deaths by being crushed.

Another infamous baby farmer, Ada Chard Williams, advertised herself as someone who specialized in finding homes for unwanted children. But rather than seeking out parents to adopt 21-month-old Selina Jones, Chard Williams battered and strangled the infant to death. When the baby's mother met Chard Williams, she didn't have the full amount to pay for her services – five pounds – but the baby farmer agreed to accept what she had on her. When the child's honest if misguided parent returned at a later date with the rest of the fee, both Chard Williams and her little girl had disappeared.

Selina's body was found soon after, washed up on the banks of the Thames at Battersea. The distinctive manner in which the little corpse had been wrapped in cloth and then the bundle tied was to prove vital in the court case in identifying Ada Chard Williams as the child's murderer. The baby farmer was hanged in March 1900 at Newgate prison. There were strong suspicions that Selina had not been her first victim, but, as with Caroline Savill, no further investigations were made, the offspring of the poorest in society having little value in the general scheme of things.

There were some who did fill a role a little closer to that of today's child-minders, and it was a service much needed by the increasing numbers of women who were being employed in jobs that took them away from their own dwellings when in the past they might have made their living doing homework. From the 1860s newspapers were carrying advertisements for women to work in jobs in the East End that were little different from those done by my aunts in the 1920s and 1930s. These included doing intricate embroidery and bead-work on evening gowns that, as James Greenwood put it, contributed 'towards the thousand and one articles that stock the fancy trade' – the poor making items that could be afforded only by the rich.

Those same newspapers carried advertisements for the baby farmers such as Ada Chard Williams, the women called by Greenwood 'mock child adopters', who would 'mind' the children while their mothers went out to work. And some of the youngsters were probably better off being taken away from their homes; the overcrowded, multiple-occupancy housing they inhabited was a breeding ground for both physical disease and moral corruption.

As Thomas Beames wrote in *The Rookeries of London*, describing life there:

> . . . *female children [fall] victims to the gross passions of abandoned men, when their tender age would have seemed to have put such dangers out of their way* . . . *when the sexes are thrown promiscuously together, do you wonder at paradoxes in immorality* . . .

By the second half of the century there would be moral, social and philanthropic campaigns concerned with what was already being spoken of by the 1860s as the sexual abuse of children. In her book on the subject, Louise A.

Jackson lists the familiar Victorian euphemisms for rape and abuse of nineteenth-century children – *molestation*, *ruining*, *causing outrage* and so on – and shows that the concept of abuse was widely recognized in the period, and was being increasingly condemned. She describes the sometimes contradictory legislation surrounding notions of sexuality in the period. These included the 1841 repeal of the death penalty for rape and the nervousness regarding the age of consent, and, perhaps most shockingly, she notes that incest was not made a criminal offence until 1908 – seven years after the death of the queen whose name is revered by those who call for a return to the values of her age.

While contemporary investigators might have been shocked by the conditions they found in the overcrowded slums, it was life in the common lodging houses that really appalled them. The worst of these were not just the cheapest way for the poor to put a temporary roof over their heads without having to resort to the work-house or to sleeping under a costermongers cart or the dripping arches of the railway viaducts; they were the training grounds for young felons and places where criminals could hide, the no-go sink estates of their day, places where even the most feared of murderers might go to ground.

5

MURDER MOST FOUL

. . . the promiscuous sale of poisons, what incredible laxity of government! One poison, indeed, has its one law. Arsenic may not be sold otherwise than coloured, nor except with full registration of the sale, and in the presence of a witness known to both buyer and vender. Admirable, so far as it goes, but why should arsenic alone receive this dab of legislation? Is the principle right, that means of murder and suicide should be rendered difficult of access for criminal purposes? Does any one question it? Then, why not legislate equally against all poisons – against oxalic acid and opium, corrosive subli-mate, strychnine . . .

Dr John Simon, *City Medical Report*, 1854

We print as a warning to all housekeepers . . . an illus-tration of episodes in connection with the startling murder of poor Mrs Wright at Canonbury in broad daylight. London residents cannot be too strongly reminded that there are wild beasts in human form about ever seeking for prey . . .

Penny Illustrated Paper, 16 May 1888

*

Looking at the above quotes, it might seem shocking to us how easily the means to murder could be had, so that the streets weren't safe even in broad daylight back in those supposedly better times. But it comes as more of a surprise to see the cavalier fashion in which murder was often dealt with by the courts – the murder of the poor, that is.

The Victorian publication *Beehive* related the sad story of the death of Anne Coney, who was murdered in 1872, concluding that, 'The crime, like many others similar in character, appeared to have been the result of drink . . . John Nagle was convicted of manslaughter and sentenced to six months imprisonment.'

Evidently, life was cheap at the lower end of the social scale, but the loss of life by murder *was* valued: as a source of popular entertainment, that is. Broadsheet sellers did excellent business with their patterers' tales of bloody murders and gory executions – the 'gallows literature' to which Mayhew refers so disparagingly and sarcastically:

The account of the trial and biography of [the murderer] his conduct in prison, etc., is a concise and clear enough condensation from the newspapers. Indeed, [his] Sorrowful Lamentation is the best, in all respects, of any execution broad-sheet I have seen; even the 'copy of verses' which, according to the established custom, the criminal composes in the condemned cell – his being unable, in some instances, to read or write being no obstacle to the composition . . . The matters of fact, however, are introduced in the same peculiar manner. The worst part is the morbid sympathy and intended apology for the criminal.

Following the removal of the final penny from newspaper duty in 1855, there was an immediate expansion of the popular press, and this was celebrated as a wonderful opportunity for the education of the working man. But newspaper proprietors soon realized what it took to increase their sales: sensation. It was as if these crimes had no real victims, but existed merely to titillate, intrigue and amuse. Maybe sensibilities have changed, or maybe we now hide our fascination behind a veneer of being appalled that such things happen and of trying to find the causes of such terrible events. Regardless of whether this is true, I found the child murders the saddest cases to research. In those involving the baby farmers there were clearly instances of terrible cruelty, but child murder could also be the final resort of the desperate: infanticide committed by those who surely needed help rather than censure.

The following report is from *The Times* of November 1873:

Yesterday afternoon it was discovered that a murder had been committed at . . . Old Gravel-lane, Wapping. The perpetrator of the deed is a man named Parker, aged about 35. He left home in the morning, telling a woman in the house he would return in a few minutes. She went upstairs soon afterwards to give the children, a boy and a girl, some food, and found both of them dead, their throats having been cut in a most brutal manner. The boy had been subject to paralysis, and the girl was a cripple. In the meantime the murderer went to the police-station and gave himself into custody. He took with him the knife with which the deed was committed. It appears that he had been in the employ of Messrs. Knight and Sons, soap-boilers and candle-makers, but for some months had wanted work and bread. He assigns as a reason for the murder utter destitution and a repugnance to allow his children to become inmates of the workhouse. The loss of his wife some time ago seems to have preyed upon his mind.

The picture we see of a father killing his child in this piece from the *Penny Illustrated Paper* is of a very different kind, and it tells us a lot that the conviction was not for murder:

William Smith, the Tunstall miner charged with the manslaughter of his stepchild, a girl three years old, by systematic ill-usage, was convicted at the Stafford Assizes. The ruffian was proved to have repeatedly kicked the child in the stomach with his clogs. Mr Justice Lush sentenced him to penal servitude for twenty years.

It seems more common for child deaths to have been the responsibility of the mothers, women who could not feed the children they already had or who had no roof over their heads to shelter their babies. The Central Middlesex coroner reported statistics showing that 800 children had been murdered in one year in that area alone, stating that the mothers were usually guilty of the crime, and that women would continue to do the same again as they were so infrequently apprehended. But as noted earlier, with no reliable contraception, overcrowded, foul conditions and no legal, or even safe illegal, abortion facilities, again, not for the poor anyway, at least some of those women must have seen infanticide as their only option – other than watching their children starve to death.

When commenting on the high incidence of infanticide at an inquest concerning 'the murder of a child by cruel exposure', Dr Lancaster, styled in the press as the 'great coroner', wanted to bring the following to public attention:

> . . . *the important subject of the great frequency of unpunished child murder . . . the most alarming feature was that the police seeing that cases of infanticide had become so common, no longer exerted themselves to discover the perpetrators of such murders . . . It was much to be feared that the public, finding that infanticide was constantly attended with impunity, would cease to regard it as a crime.*

A police officer present at the same court hearing commented:

> . . . *the railway arches were so often used to deposit bodies that special watches were set, but upon one occasion, within two hours after a search had been made, the body of a murdered child was*

deposited there. In the case immediately under consideration it was
proved that the deceased had been placed naked on the ground near
the arches of the Metropolitan railway, and that it had died from
the cold.

Meanwhile, the body of a baby girl dead from head injuries
found in Hoxton Square, wrapped in a canvas grocer's sack,
had another coroner expressing the hope that 'The discovery
and punishment of the offenders in even one such case
might do much to check the shocking practice of child
murder . . . However, he was not optimistic, and how right
he was.

One of the most enduring images of child murder from
the period was that of 'sweet Fanny Adams', of Alton,
Hampshire, who was killed not by a parent but by a stranger
who abducted her. It was half past one on a glorious
Saturday afternoon in August 1867, and eight-year-old
Fanny, her little sister Lizzie and their friend Minnie Warner
were approached by a man who said he'd give Lizzie and
Minnie some money for sweets if they went off to play,
and that he'd give Fanny a halfpenny if she stayed with
him. When the others were about to leave, Fanny became
unsure about remaining with the stranger, but the man
picked her up and carried her off to a nearby hop garden.
When Minnie and Lizzie returned home at around five
o'clock and spoke about the man and his kind gifts, Fanny's
mother and a neighbour hurried off to search for the child.
They came across a man walking towards them and

demanded to know if he was the person who had given money to the children. He answered that he was and that he was in a habit of doing so. He explained further that he was a clerk with a local solicitor and then, having proved his respectability, he went on his way. Two hours later, Fanny was still missing, but unfortunately not for long. At around seven o'clock, one of the neighbours who had joined the search party looking for the child came across part of a brutally mutilated and butchered body.

That evening, when the police arrested Frederick Baker, the 29-year-old clerk who had identified himself to Mrs Adams and her neighbour, he denied his part in the crime, despite the fact that he was spattered with blood, his boots and trouser bottoms were wet, as if they had recently been washed, and he was carrying two knives. There were also witnesses that Baker had been absent from his place of work between one and three twenty-five, and had gone out again at about five, which fitted in with the times he had approached the girls and when he had later spoken with Mrs Adams and her neighbour. The likelihood was that he had first murdered the child and then returned to the scene to carry out the mutilation of the body. A colleague of Baker's reinforced the police's growing suspicions, stating that when the search was on Baker had said it would be awkward for him if the child was found murdered and that he would probably leave the area very soon. He also claimed that Baker said he could start a new career and 'go as a butcher'. What clinched it for the police was the diary entry they found when they searched his desk: '24th August, Saturday – killed a young girl. It was fine and hot.'

Following Baker's committal for trial, the police had to fight against a furious mob that had gathered to attack him, a scene which evokes modern-day images of crowds – predominantly enraged women – rocking prison vans as suspected murderers are driven in and out of the courts where they are standing trial. When Baker was hanged in front of a crowd that exceeded 5,000 people, even though the punishment was carried out at eight o'clock in the morning on Christmas Eve 1867, it was reported that much of the crowd was also female – women screaming for rough justice.

There are macabre hangovers from the murder of the little eight-year-old girl. Soon after the terrible events, the Royal Navy's sailors were issued with a new, not much appreciated convenience food – tinned mutton – and it quickly became known as Sweet Fanny Adams, due to the look and texture of the contents. And, as time passed, 'sweet F.A.' came to be a polite way of saying 'sweet fuck all', meaning 'nothing'.

A murderer whose deeds are surprisingly not *more* remembered is Mary Ann Cotton, a con woman and biga-mist who was finally hanged in 1873 for the death of a young boy. Using a series of false names and details, Mary Ann moved around the country, leaving behind her at least twenty-one dead bodies. The deaths included those of three of her four husbands, at least one lover, her mother, many of her thirteen children and various stepchildren. She benefited from their deaths by making life insurance claims, inheriting their goods and releasing herself from the bother of having to care for unwanted babies. Suspicion had fallen on Mary several times following the deaths of people close to her, as she seemed to have a remarkable talent for predicting that somebody would soon die, regardless of the current state of their health. But at a time when medical care was a hit-or-miss affair and infant mortality so high, she was given the benefit of the doubt and death certificates were signed despite reservations that something untoward was happening. It was only when one of Mary's stepsons died that a doctor became doubtful enough to refuse to give his signature and a post-mortem was carried out. The examination revealed arsenic in the child's stomach. Mary Ann Cotton was accused, found guilty and sentenced to be hanged. The execution had to be postponed until after the birth of yet another child.

As the black flag was flying above Durham prison to show the hanging had taken place, hawkers were doing good business selling photographs of the now notorious woman. It was never proved just how many of the deaths resulted from Mary Ann's propensity for murder, but modern-day criminologists have suggested that her profile classifies her as what would be known now as a serial killer.

Even following the widespread publicity given to such executions, the death sentence seemed to have had little deterrent effect on women determined to rid themselves of inconvenient people. Towards the end of Victoria's reign there was the case of Mary Eleanor Wheeler, a young woman who chose to be known as Pearcey, the name of an ex-lover. Ironically she chose to use another surname because her real one might have led people to associate her with her father, a man who himself had been hanged for murder when Mary was still a teenager.

The self-styled Mary Pearcey had a series of lovers, one of whom was Frank Hogg. Hogg had married a woman called Phoebe when she became pregnant with their daughter, at the same time as he was having a relationship with Mary. His marriage didn't stop the liaison with Mary and he continued to visit his mistress regularly at her home in Kentish Town.

In October 1890 Mary sent a lad with a note inviting Phoebe Hogg to come and have tea with her. She had developed what appeared to be a warm friendship with Phoebe to cover up the affair she was having with the woman's husband. Mrs Hogg and her little girl – also called Phoebe – went to visit Mary. Neither of them was ever seen alive again. That evening a woman's body was found in Hampstead, her throat slashed and her head battered. Later that night a blood-smeared perambulator was found by a police officer and the next day the body of a little girl was discovered. She had been suffocated. After learning of the grisly discoveries, Frank panicked about the absence of his wife and child and went to the police, while on his instructions his sister visited Mary to ask if she'd seen anything of Mrs Hogg. While there, Frank's sister asked Mary to accompany her to the mortuary to see if the body that had been found was Phoebe's.

Following a positive identification, Frank Hogg became the obvious suspect and his home was searched, but Mary Pearcey's behaviour at the mortuary had been odd enough to have alerted Hogg's sister and the police officers who had been present. When, during his interrogation by the police, Hogg admitted that Mary Pearcey was his mistress, officers were dispatched to Kentish Town to interview her and search her home. Bizarrely, while they looked around the house, Mary sat at the piano playing, singing and whistling, and calmly stating that all the blood in the kitchen and the signs of violent struggle were the result of her attempts to get rid of an infestation of mice. The police quickly unravelled the ludicrous story and it was revealed that Mary had murdered Mrs Hogg and then suffocated the little girl, probably by putting her in the pram and stuffing her mother's dead body on top of her. Mary Pearcey was executed at Newgate two days before Christmas in 1890. Madame Tussaud's exhibited a wax model of the murderer alongside the pram, which Frank Hogg had sold to them.

But, as we have already seen in the short extract from the *Beehive* quoted earlier where a killer was sentenced to just six months' imprisonment, not all murderers were executed. An earlier Victorian killer who, like Mary Pearcey, committed an act of *crime passionel* was Christiana Edmunds, the infamous Brighton Poisoner.

In 1871 Christiana had become obsessed with a local medical practitioner, Dr Beard, but alas, like Frank Hogg, the doctor was a married man. Deciding that Mrs Beard was the only thing standing in the way of her happiness, Christiana set about getting rid of her in what became an increasingly complicated and bizarre manner. First, she purchased a quantity of strychnine from Isaac Garret, a chemist and dentist of Queens Road, claiming that she wanted to poison some stray cats that were bothering her, and then she injected the poison into some chocolate creams she had bought from Maynard's, a confectioner and lozenge maker in West Street. She offered one of the sweets to Dr Beard's wife, who spat it out because of the unpleasant taste, but she had ingested enough of the poison to make her ill. Panicking that she would be accused of attempting to murder the woman and so lose her chance of living happily ever after with the doctor, Christiana thought it wise to implicate someone else in the crime and so she set about framing Mr Maynard, the confectioner. She waited near the man's shop until a child came along who was willing to run an errand for her. She then sent the child into the shop to buy more chocolates, which she took home and injected randomly with strychnine. She then found another helpful child to return the chocolates to Maynard's on the pretext that they were the wrong type, swapping them for another sort. The helpful shopkeeper exchanged the chocolates as requested and then returned the original purchase back to his stock. From then on, he was innocently selling poisoned confectionery to the people of Brighton. Several of them fell ill and one little boy, Sidney Barker, actually died. Following his death, Christiana failed to realize that the next steps in her plan to avoid detection were to be her undoing. She went on a campaign of sending poisoned fruits and foodstuffs to people around the town, and to herself – going to the police with a complaint that she was one of the victims under attack from the poisoner. She also sent letters of accusation to the sweet-shop owner and a letter to the child's father suggesting the cause of the little boy's death. The letters were all traced back to her.

When Christiana was tried and found guilty of the crime, evidence was given of recurring insanity within her family, as a result of which the death penalty was withdrawn. She died in Broadmoor in 1907, six years after the death of Queen Victoria.

There was no such excuse for the murderer described in this 1862 piece from the *Penny Illustrated Paper*, despite the journals claim that he was maddened, and their view that the case was 'sad' is open to interpretation, it being unclear whether we should feel sorry for the murderer or his victim.

A sad case of murder was brought before the Thames police magistrate on Tuesday. A labourer named Samuel Howard, after coming home from a hard day's work, found the woman, Sarah Smith, with whom he cohabitated, in a state of intoxication, and no food provided for him. Maddened by these circumstances, he knocked the woman

*down, and kicked and beat her till she died, and then went to sleep
with the mangled body of the victim in the room. In the morning he
called in the police, when he was taken in to custody.*

Some murderers became such celebrities that their names
are as familiar to us now as they were to our nineteenth-
century forebears. Jack the Ripper is the obvious one, but
there was also Franz Müller. This might seem unlikely – who
has ever heard of him? But as can be seen in the glossary
at the back of this book, 'muller' is a slang word used by
East Enders meaning to murder – as in the bloodthirsty,
'I'll muller you!' It has now evolved in younger Londoners'
slang to mean being drunk – as in 'he was mullered', meaning
'he was slaughtered'. It seems likely that the word was
adopted into the language because of the sensational
publicity that appeared across the media, from the daily
press to the penny broadsheets, much as a modern catch-
phrase is now taken up and repeated from popular
television shows, eventually becoming common usage. In
this instance, the events of the case even triggered a craze
in hat fashions. This can all be traced back to the man who
carried out the first murder on a British railway train, namely
Franz Müller.

From the opening of the world's first public railway – the
Stockton and Darlington – in 1825 criminals were quick to
see the potential in the new transport system. Rather than
robbing horse-drawn-carriage passengers of their luggage
and possessions, they could now turn their attention to

those travelling on trains. As the trains originally had no interlinking corridors between the usually unlit compartments, they would be plunged into isolating deepest darkness when going through tunnels, providing near-perfect conditions for those with ill intent – whether planning robbery or assault – against fellow passengers. In France, four years before the Müller incident, a robbery victim on a train was shot dead, and there were spates of reports abhorring all railway crimes, but it wasn't until the Müller case that the press really went into a frenzy as they reported on the death of Mr Thomas Briggs, an almost seventy-year-old chief clerk in a City bank, as this, importantly, was to be the first railway murder in *England*.

It was late on the evening of 9 July 1864, in Hackney, and two young clerks entered an empty carriage on a train coming from the direction of Fenchurch Street. When one of them sat in a pool of what he quickly realized was blood they alerted the guard, who, with the aid of a lamp, literally threw light on to the scene. What they discovered was a great deal of blood, and also a hat, a walking cane and a bag, the last two of which were established as belonging to a Mr Thomas Briggs. The beaver hat that was found in the carriage, however, was not the property of the habitually top-hat-wearing gentleman. When the unfortunate man's body was located by the side of the line between Hackney Wick and Bow stations, the chase for his killer was on.

It was an impressive piece of detection. Guessing that

this was a robbery, as the body didn't have the expected watch and chain across the waistcoat, Chief Inspector Tanner of Scotland Yard first concentrated on speaking to jewellers, as they might have bought the items from the killer. The stolen property was tracked down to an establishment on Cheapside in the City of London, where the proprietor, John Death, was able to furnish a description of the man who had brought it in. The next break came from a cabman who, reading about the murder, came forward to say that he had information that might be of help. His ten-year-old daughter had recently been given a box bearing the distinctive name Death by a young German, a man to whom his older daughter had, at the time, been engaged. He also had information on the beaver hat, which linked it to Franz Müller, and, a further vital clue, he had a photograph of the man, given by Müller to his daughter. The photograph was identified by the jeweller as being a likeness of the man who had sold him what he now knew to be the watch and chain stolen from the late Thomas Briggs.

Despite all the expert, and also lucky, investigative work, there was a snag: it was discovered that Müller had left England on 15 July – six days after the attack – bound for New York aboard the passenger ship *Victoria*. But the police weren't about to give up. They took a faster ship across the Atlantic, the SS *City of Manchester*, arriving in New York just shy of three weeks before Müller. On his arrest, the young German was found to be in possession of the top hat belonging to Mr Briggs, the crown of which he had cut down and lowered to disguise it.

Returning to England for trial, Müller protested his innocence, the defence bringing forward witnesses, including a prostitute who claimed to have been with him at the time of the murder, and stated that the beaver hat was in fact the property of the cabman who had been so 'helpful' to the police. But the jury weren't impressed with his story and Müller was sentenced to be publicly hanged on 14 November 1864.

Müller left several legacies. As well as his name entering the language, albeit as slang, copies of his foreshortened hat became a fad among fashion-conscious young men for a while. More seriously, the behaviour of the rowdy, drunken crowd at his execution was so deplorable that it contributed to the growing body of opinion that was arguing against treating hangings as ghoulish public entertainment.

In the same year that Franz Müller achieved notoriety, the father of Henry Wainwright died, leaving his son – also called Henry – a large inheritance. Superficially, a successful, well-liked individual, the younger Wainwright seemed to be the epitome of industrious Victorian respectability. He worked hard, carrying on the family's brush-making business on the Whitechapel Road, which was situated next door to the 'Pav', the popular Pavilion Theatre, while he and his wife and children lived in Tredegar Square – still grand today – behind the Bow Road.

Wainwright was keen on the Pav and would have entertainers from the various shows visit him at home. Unfortunately for Mrs Wainwright, Henry had a particular interest in the female performers and would organize secret liaisons with them, and probably not for the purpose of discussing theatre and the dramatic arts. But when he met Harriet Lane, an apprentice milliner rather than an entertainer, his head was turned completely. She was pretty, educated and young, and Henry went a bit further this time than just showing an interest. Unbeknownst to his wife, he set up a second household. The couple moved around from East End to West End and back again, with young Harriet bearing her lover two daughters along the way. But the fickle Mr Wainwright came to a decision that he had had enough of Harriet, not least because his finances were becoming rather stretched by his unusual family arrangements. He came up with a plan. He would introduce Harriet to his brother Thomas – for some reason giving him the pseudonym Teddy Frieake – who would woo her and then pretend to take her off his hands. But even though Harriet had by now succumbed to drink and was living in lodgings and was not that bothered about who was keeping her – so long as somebody did – it didn't work out as Harriet had expected. The day she was supposed to move in with Henry's brother was the last time she was seen alive.

What actually happened to her was that she was shot, battered and mutilated before being buried under Wainwright's warehousing premises, close to his brush-making factory on the Whitechapel Road. Unfortunately for

Wainwright, though, getting rid of his mistress didn't help his finances. In 1875 he was declared bankrupt, and the warehouse lease had to be sold on to new tenants. Unluckier still for Wainwright, the body of Harriet Lane, buried under the warehouse floor, was now noticeably rank. He had to act fast, or he might become incriminated in the death of a woman he had claimed was living abroad. So he decided to shift the remains elsewhere before the new tenants moved in and investigated the stench. He would then reinter the body in Borough High Street, where his brother had an ironmonger's. After cutting his dead lover into manageable-sized pieces, Henry wrapped the bits in tidy parcels. He then asked a somewhat reluctant young lad, Alf Stokes, a one-time employee of his, to help him ferry the foul-smelling packages out on to the Whitechapel Road and then to keep an eye on them while he went to fetch a cab. It is not clear why the foolish man didn't send Alf for the cab, but it was to be the beginning of his downfall.

While Henry was off seeking transport, Alf's curiosity got the better of him and he couldn't resist having a sneaky look at what was stinking so badly He must have regretted it, because what he uncovered was a human hand. By the time Wainwright returned in a cab, Alf had managed to conceal his discovery, but Henry probably wouldn't have noticed anyway as his conviction of the brilliance of his plan had clearly gone to his head. Almost unbelievably, Wainwright had invited a young woman, Alice Day – variously described in the court reports as a dressmaker, a ballerina and a chorus girl from the Pav – to join him on the journey, while he puffed on a cigar to disguise the stench.

As Wainwright, his artistic companion and the remains of his one-time mistress made off in the direction of the Borough, the appalled Alfred Stokes sprinted behind, all the while trying to find a constable to arrest the murderer. Again, in an almost implausible twist, Alf's story was mocked by the first two policemen he encountered, who declared him to be a madman. And so he decided there was nothing for it, he would just have to carry on in pursuit – even legging it hot foot through the traffic across London Bridge to keep up – until at last the cab came to a halt outside the ironmonger's on Borough High Street.

This time Alf found two officers who were willing to listen to his story and they demanded to see the contents of the parcels. Ever confident, Wainwright refused, and had the bare-faced cheek to offer them a bribe. As the court report in *The Times* had it: 'Say nothing, ask no questions, and there's £50 each for you.' The constables were not so easily corrupted and, despite the size of the proposed back-hander, they turned down his offer. The contents of the parcels were revealed and Wainwright, Alice Day and Harriet's mortal remains were all removed to Stone's End police station.

Henry was hanged on 21 December 1875 – according to *The Times*, he 'died hard', a horrible description of a terrible act. Alfred Stokes was rewarded with £30 from public funds, while Alice went on to become something of a celebrity and principal dancer at the Pav.

Rather more successful than Wainwright – for a while – was Dr Thomas Neill Cream, who came to be known as the Lambeth Poisoner. In the course of his criminal career he would eventually be charged twice with murder. Glaswegian-born Cream can be categorically held responsible for five deaths, but it is very likely that he was guilty of many more than those for which he was convicted, as his killing spree began well before he reached Lambeth.

Raised and educated in Canada, Cream graduated in medicine and was then forced by his pregnant girlfriend's family to marry her – after almost killing the young woman when he performed a botched abortion on her. After the wedding, Cream immediately moved to Britain, leaving his wife behind. He spent some time working in Edinburgh – as a doctor and illegal abortionist – where another young woman became pregnant by him. She was found dead in what were thought to be suspicious circumstances and Dr Cream fled back across the Atlantic, this time relocating to Chicago, where there was a failed attempt to prosecute him when a prostitute died as the result of yet another messed-up termination.

He wouldn't be so lucky the next time, when he used strychnine to do away with a man named Daniel Stott. The story varies between the protagonists' versions as to whether Cream was Stott's wife's lover or, as Mrs Stott claimed, it was her husband and not her who was having an affair. But whoever was telling the truth, what Cream did next shows that either he was less clever than he believed or he was an attention-seeking egomaniac; the second seems the more likely, considering his subsequent behaviour. Cream actually wrote to the authorities suggesting that Stott's body should be exhumed and examined for traces of poison. They did so, and when Cream and Mrs Stott were consequently arrested, his mistress decided to save herself by offering to give evidence that would incriminate the doctor but not herself. Mrs Stott was let off, but Cream wasn't so fortunate. He was sentenced to life in Joliet. Rather oddly, he was released after just ten years and there were rumours of bribes being paid, something not unheard of under the prison's then notoriously corrupt regime. He wasted no time in moving on once again, on this occasion to the place that would earn him his nickname the Lambeth Poisoner. Between his arrival in October 1891 and his capture in June 1892, Cream was responsible for what would have been the agonizing, convulsive deaths by strychnine poisoning of at least four prostitutes: Matilda Clover, Ellen Donworth, Alice Marsh and Emma Showell. The streets of London were filled with fear that Jack the Ripper had returned to his slaughtering ways, but had just crossed the river to a different red-light district and was using an alternative method of doing away with the 'brides'. Being a tough area, the part of Lambeth in which Cream was operating – in every sense – attracted people who didn't necessarily wish to be traced or identified, and there might well have been many more victims who will remain forever unknown.

If only Cream had learned from the behaviour which led to his previous conviction and just kept quiet, he might have got away with his crimes, but he didn't – or maybe he couldn't. He did several strange things, including circulating a letter among the guests of the Metropole Hotel, claiming that the murderer of Ellen Donworth worked there and if they didn't leave immediately all their lives would be in danger. He also tried to blame another doctor for the women's deaths, all the while bragging about his knowledge of the case, going so far as to take several people on a walking tour of the sites of the murders. Regrettably for Cream, one of the people to whom he showed the crime scenes and shared his wealth of information was a police officer. The doctor was put under surveillance and was soon arrested.

Cream was hanged on 15 November 1892, and in what some say was a final moment of bravado, but others believe to be the solution to an enduring mystery, his last words before the noose tightened around his neck were said to have been, 'I am Jack the . . .'

The controversy remains as to whether Cream could have been the Ripper. The dates of the Whitechapel murders clash with his time in Joliet for one thing, but there have been various arguments trying to explain this away. One is that the doctor had a double with whom he worked for many years, but as he was markedly cross-eyed, it must have been quite a coincidence coming across even a reasonable look-alike. Another is that he was able to pay to leave the corrupt Joliet many years before his official release was ever announced and that he lived in London in anonymity, performing illegal abortions and murdering prostitutes. When we consider Jack the Rippers career and some of the suggested suspects in the next chapter, such theories might seem as likely as any of the others.

Another murderous doctor who would probably now find himself being labelled as a serial killer was Dr William Palmer, known as the Rugeley Poisoner. Although Palmer was convicted and hanged for the murder of just one person, John Parsons Cook, it is believed that he murdered up to a further dozen, if not more victims, including one of his debtors, his own children, his well-off mother-in-law, his wife and brother. He was actually found guilty of the latter two deaths by a coroner's court.

Palmer was a popular man who unfortunately developed a gambling habit that he wasn't able to support. He also had a liking for women who went on to blackmail him, but he never had much of a sense of financial responsibility. His way of life found him with a young family, a pile of debts and creditors approaching him with increasingly worrying threats, demanding that he repay his many outstanding bills immediately.

A typical compulsive gambler, Palmer thought that the big win – the answer to all his problems – was just around the corner. Over a series of nine days in November 1855, Palmer kept company with Cook, a racehorse owner he had befriended. They visited the races, where Palmer's bets all failed to come up with the solution he was seeking so desperately, but Cook's horse won a major handicap that carried a large purse. He threw a dinner to celebrate. Over the next few days the men spent a great deal of time together. Cook then fell ill, and despite Dr Palmer prescribing various treatments for him, the man became progressively sicker, eventually dying on 21 November in convulsive agony.

Cooks stepfather did not trust Palmer and called for an investigation into the death. When a toxicologist at Guys Hospital performed an autopsy and declared that John Parsons Cook had died as a result of antimony poisoning, the suspicions were put together with the clues and Palmer was arrested. He was convicted of his supposed friend's murder at the Old Bailey and was publicly hanged on 14 June 1856, in front of a crowd of 30,000 people. His wax effigy was to be displayed in the Chamber of Horrors at Madame Tussaud's for over 120 years.

Another Victorian murderer, Kate Webster, not only did away with her victim but was also accused of being responsible for turning the victim's neighbours into unwitting cannibals.

In January 1879 Kate, an Irish-born petty thief and minor fraudster with a child to raise, found herself a live-in job as a servant to Mrs Julia Martha Thomas, a widow, at the woman's home in Richmond. It didn't take long for Mrs Thomas, known as a difficult person at the best of times, to begin complaining about the laziness of her new employee, and the relationship between the two women soured rapidly Things came to a head just a few weeks later, in February, when Kate was given notice to leave, which meant she would be homeless and unable to pay the woman who was minding her child.

By the first Sunday in March the time had come for Kate to leave. As usual Mrs Thomas attended religious services both in the morning and in the evening. What happened on her return from the latter was to result in the sorry end of both women. Kate had decided that the way out of her difficulties with her employer was to murder her, and so she did, but rather than stealing what she could and fleeing the scene of her crime, instead she dismembered, boiled and burned the body with the intention of disposing of the remains in the river.

Kate worked hard for the next few days, scrubbing and clearing away all traces of her crime, but she was left with two problems – the head and one foot of her victim, which she couldn't fit into the box in which she'd stowed the rest of Mrs Thomas. Her solution was to dump the foot on a rubbish heap and to hide the head in a bag. But Kate began to get over-confident and started to draw attention to herself by wearing her dead employer's clothing. She then went around the neighbourhood, trying to sell the rest of the woman's possessions. To those who knew Mrs Thomas, Kate merely stated that she had gone away, and to those who did not know her, Kate claimed she had recently inherited the house and its contents from an aunt. Her increasingly bold behaviour was to precipitate a series of events that would ultimately result in her being found out.

It was reported that a box containing a body, minus the head and one foot, had been found washed up on the banks of the Thames. A young man who had been recruited by Kate to help her carry a box became worried that it was the same one, and that he might have been unknowingly assisting her in a crime. He therefore came forward with information. Then there was the neighbour who was wondering what was going on next door as she watched Kate flogging off all her employer's worldly goods – apart from the ones she had taken to wearing. And where was Mrs Thomas? Kate decided that it was time to take the money and flee back home. But the final blow came when police searched the house and found fragments of charred human remains, as well as tools that could have been used for chopping and slicing the body. Kate was tracked down in Ireland and arrested for murder.

Following her execution, on 29 July 1879 at Wandsworth prison, it was probably the accusation that, after boiling Mrs Thomas, Kate had transferred the rendered human fat into pots and had then sold them to her victim's neighbours as dripping which gave her sufficient notoriety to become another long-term fixture in Madame Tussaud's Chamber of Horrors.

There were many more murder cases that occurred throughout Victoria's supposedly so agreeable reign, crimes resulting from desperation, theft, anger, greed, drunken brawls, passion and insanity. But not all the murders were explained, not all of them were even noticed and certainly not all of them were solved. There would be one series of murders, however, that would become the iconic crime of the whole century and that still continues to appal and fascinate to this day. These, of course, are the Whitechapel murders that took place in the autumn of 1888.

6

1888 – JACK'S REIGN OF TERROR

Commercial Street, the broad thoroughfare linking Whitechapel to Shoreditch, had been built in a grand moment of Victorian moralising, optimism and innovation. Designed to slice its way through one of the East Ends most notorious rookeries, the idealistic intention behind its creation was the sweeping away of overcrowding, disease and corruption, in the foul and crime-ridden slums that were so uncomfortably close to the City of London – the fabulously wealthy hub of the greatest Empire ever seen. The road would literally open up the area to the light, making it available for inspection by authorities and worthies alike, allowing them to check on the feckless underclasses, who lived on their very doorstep.

Just thirty years after its completion the world's gaze would again be focussed on the area. Not to admire the social and environmental improvements, but to be appalled and stunned by the brutal acts of the proto-serial killer known as Jack the Ripper, and consequently on the shameful, persistent presence of such grotesque poverty and depravity.

The bold new road had proved itself embarrassingly worthy of its name, as a shocked public realized that commerce of many different kinds took place in its shadowy environs, and, despite the best intentions and interventions of the Establishment, they would long continue to do so.

Gilda O'Neill, *The Sins of Their Fathers*, 2002

*

The year 1887 might have seen the commemoration of Victoria's Golden Jubilee, but generally the mid-1880s were not a time for celebration. The winter of 1885 – 6 had seen the worst weather in living memory, causing distress in both town and country. Snow fell from October right though until May, and in January, in just seven hours, a full foot of it fell on the capital. There was massive and escalating unemployment. Fear of mob violence was gripping the middling classes, while there were worries about the increasing radicalism among the labouring classes, as violence, riots and strikes were breaking out. There was worsening overcrowding in the slums and a rise in the numbers of homeless. In addition to this, a vicious campaign of anti-Semitism was being directed at the growing numbers of Jewish refugees who were fleeing to Britain to escape from the murderous pogroms of Tsarist Russia. All of these events, with their potential for sensationalism, were pounced on as great copy by the press. But despite all the fears and disturbances, by the August of 1888 – a far more than averagely eventful year, as William Fishman has shown in his book named for that year – they would pale into insignificance as it was realized that a serial killer had unleashed his wrath in the east of the capital.

He would terrorize the people of London and beyond, capturing and horrifying the imagination of the public right around the world. The Whitechapel murders would, open a window on to another side of life, one that many Victorians had either not known existed or had simply refused to acknowledge was there. This was despite the evidence of their own eyes, as they nightly witnessed the hordes of desperate people sleeping rough in the royal parks and in Trafalgar Square, right in the midst of what had been until then the comfortably complacent West End.

There continues to be wide speculation, wild theories and passionate argument surrounding the events of that autumn of 1888, mostly regarding the identity of the murderer, who had come to be known as Jack the Ripper. As well as contemporary reports, both official and otherwise, and the many books dedicated to the subject – from the ludicrous to the scholarly – there are numerous websites favouring one theory or another. One of the most thorough, which brings much of the material and references together, can be found in *Casebook: Jack the Ripper* at www.casebook.org.

But to begin with, putting aside the identity of the killer, there isn't even any agreement as to how many victims there were. Some extreme, self-styled 'Ripper-ologists' have speculated that over thirty women were murdered by the Ripper, while others contend that there were as few as three. Obviously three is still an appalling tally – one would have been too many – but nothing like as shocking. The general consensus, though, is that there were five victims. The first was Mary Ann Nichols, known in the Victorian tradition as Polly – as was my own Victorian grandmother, who always held that the Ripper was, in fact, a woman, a midwife driven to madness by the seemingly endless abortions she had carried out for the 'brides'. The other four are thought to have been Annie Chapman, Elizabeth Stride, Catherine Eddowes and Mary Jane Kelly – with the deaths of Elizabeth Stride and Catherine Eddowes being known as the double killing, as they occurred on the same night. The evidence can just about be stretched to include Emma Smith and Martha Tabram, who both died before Polly Nichols – the first of the so-called canonical five – as it can for Rose Mylett, 'Clay Pipe' Alice McKenzie, and Frances Coles, who died after Mary Jane Kelly, the last of the five. Some of these have been dismissed because they weren't killed at the weekend, which would spoil the theory that the murderer was a butcher from the continental cattle boats that docked in the Thames late on Thursday evenings and left by Monday morning.

Another incident that some have claimed must have been

the work of Jack the Ripper is reported in the following piece from the *Penny Illustrated Paper* of 24 November 1888, under the headline 'Fresh East-End Outrage'. The method of the attempted murder seems close to that used on the generally accepted five victims, and the area in which the attack took place is well within that favoured by the killer.

An outrage . . . was committed last Wednesday [at] about four o'clock in the morning, a man, and a woman named Farmer, of the unfortunate class, engaged a bed at a common lodging-house in George-street, Spitalfields. The man suddenly made an attempt to cut his companion's throat. The woman screamed loudly for assistance. Her throat was only slightly wounded, so that she was able to exert all her strength in coping with her assailant. He hastily fled the house. Meanwhile the screaming had attracted a few persons to the locality. These gave chase to the fugitive . . . [but] the man disappeared somewhere, it is said, in the direction of Heneage-street . . . she gave [a] detailed description of her assailant as follows:- age about thirty, height 5ft 6in . . . the woman who had so fortunately escaped is between forty and fifty years of age . . . [she] declares that the same man accosted her twelve months ago.

Despite the fact that the day of the week did not fit with the usual modus operandi, both the assailant's and the potential victim's descriptions fit well with those seen in the pattern of evidence presented in the principal five killings. The question has to be asked: did the writer of the report *make* the facts fit? But at least the artists responsible for the press sketches of the victims did not do them the injustice of prettifying and tidying them up to make them better copy.

Unlike the representations of the women who died so horribly that are shown in popular films and described in novels, the victims were not bright young beautiful things, but were drunks in their late thirties and forties. They were living impoverished lives in every sense: separated from their families and with few possessions other than the clothes they stood up in and the few paltry items they could secrete about their persons, keeping them safe from the fingers of thieves mean enough to steal from those as poor, or even poorer, than themselves. In Polly Nichols's pocket – a drawstring affair that could be tied around the waist under the overskirt for a measure of security – all that was found was a comb, a handkerchief and a scrap of looking glass. There was no money, which confirmed that she didn't have the means to pay for her stay in the common lodging house on the night she was killed. The cost of a stay in the spike would have been 8d for a double bed, if she had to bring back a 'customer' and had wanted to share – despite there being no privacy except maybe a curtain, 4d if she had wanted or could have afforded the luxury of a single; or 2d if she didn't object to trying to sleep on a hard wooden bench, while she draped her arms and chest over a rope stretched across the room. But poor, deranged Polly had been confident enough to boast to the keeper of the common lodging house, the man who'd thrown her out on to the street on the last evening she was ever seen alive, that getting a few coppers wouldn't be a problem for the likes of her. 'See what a jolly bonnet I've got,' she was heard bragging, believing that the hat added so much to her booze-raddled looks that she'd soon be able to earn the price of a place to rest her head and would be back in no time at all to snore the drunken night away. Sadly, it wasn't to be.

The inventory of Catherine Eddowes's possessions, excluding her clothes, might be a little longer, but it makes for equally heartbreaking reading. She had two handkerchiefs; twelve pieces of rag; a piece of white coarse linen; a piece of blue and white shirting; two small bags made from bed ticking; a couple of clay pipes; a small tin box containing tea and another containing sugar; a bit of flannel; six little bits of soap; a comb; a blunt table knife; a spoon; a cigarette case; an empty matchbox; a piece of flannel wrapped around some pins and needles; a ball of hemp [twine]; and a bit of an old apron. Perhaps even more movingly, she was also in possession of the remains of a pair of broken spectacles; a single red mitten; and an old mustard tin containing two pawn tickets, neither of which was made out in her name. These women were victims long before their deaths.

The murders were characterized by a cut to the throat which was deep enough to sever the carotid artery, leading to a quick, almost instantaneous death – explaining why the women were not able to scream to attract attention or even to call out for help – and then the killer performed the series of mutilations for which he became so feared as well as so famous. The women showed no evident signs of being the victims of rape, but it is difficult to see how such injuries could have resulted from anything other than sexually motivated violence, and modern-day speculation, based on profiling techniques, has described the killer as being triggered by exactly such a drive. There is also a widespread belief that the Ripper carried out various rituals at the crime scenes, including placing items around the body, some of which, it was claimed, were associated with Freemasonry. But such acts and links have been dismissed as the inventions of over-enthusiastic Victorian journalists hoping to sell extra copies.

As time went by and the killer was not apprehended, there was a mounting and widespread feeling of unease – reaching as far as the Queen herself – that the police force weren't doing their job. Understandable at the time, when London was being terrorized, but why should we be surprised by their failure? The view then was that the murders must have been committed by some sort of insane, sub-human monster, while today psychologists suggest that serial killers present themselves as being outwardly rather ordinary people, certainly not the person who would be the first you'd suspect. But as this wasn't the attitude at the time, there were those who went so far as to blame Richard Mansfield, the actor who was astonishing audiences with his portrayal of Jekyll and Hyde on the London stage, for inflaming the passions of the lunatic killer. And despite the

Victorians' self-belief in their scientific and technological abilities – resulting in no little measure from their acquisitions and achievements throughout the Empire, and their astonishing accomplishments of industrialization – they were hardly equipped to carry out sophisticated investigations. Some of their techniques now seem more like voodoo, as no doubt our present-day efforts will appear to those in the future. There was one belief that an image of a killer would be somehow captured in the eye of the victim during their dying moments and that a photograph of the eye could then be taken to reveal the identity of the culprit. There is no evidence, however, only conjecture, as to whether the technique was ever employed in the search for Whitechapel Jack, but other less 'scientific', more amateur methods were certainly employed.

The Whitechapel Vigilance Committee, for instance, was organized by local traders and residents concerned to protect their neighbourhood, which was under threat from the fiend, and it offered a reward payable to anyone helping to identify the culprit, even though the Home Office failed to do so. An angry juror at one of the women's inquests accused the government of class prejudice, stating that if the victims had been from the West End rather than the east, a reward would have been offered without delay. One MP, Samuel Montague, a wealthy philanthropist known for his work in the East End, did help – unlike his colleagues in the Home Office or the police force. His efforts were recorded in the *Illustrated Police News* of 22 September:

The report that in their anxiety to bring the criminal to justice the members of H Division of police had subscribed £50 to supplement the reward of £100 offered by Mr Samuel Montague, M.P., is unfounded. The police of this division entertain hopes that the private offer of a reward of £100 may lead many of those who are frequenters of the common lodging-houses in the neighbourhood, and have hitherto been reluctant to give information, to come forward and give evidence which may materially facilitate the work of the officers engaged in unravelling the mystery.

The same edition had a cover depicting otherwise respectable-looking women armed with guns, knives and coshes for self-defence, women who obviously had little confidence that the law would protect them. Another suggestion came from a journalist who put out a call for any boxers living in or near the area where the murders had happened to volunteer themselves to get done up in drag – a term in use in Victorian times, probably because of the way women's clothes dragged on the ground. Being dressed as women meant that they would not alarm or alert the killer as they patrolled the streets and so could more easily apprehend him. The journalist added that the befrocked boxers could hardly do worse than the local coppers.

In what does sound very like desperation, the police commissioner, Sir Charles Warren, decided that a pair of trained bloodhounds should be brought in to track down the beast. The commissioners diminishing reputation fell even further, and the press, who already had it in for him over his failure to catch the culprit, now mocked him for thinking it was a sensible idea to unleash a pair of blood-hounds in the courts and alley-ways of the East End. There was even a false story circulated in the newspapers that the wretched creatures, obviously not up to the job in the big city, had lost themselves on Tooting Common in the thick London fog.

So the locals were being terrorized, and anger was esca-lating at the lack of official response, and members of the police force themselves also realized what was going on. As Charles Clarkson, a retired police officer with over thirty years' service, and J. Hall, a journalist, wrote in an 1889 article called 'Police!':

> *It is rather a discouraging reflection to recall that in the year 1888, when Spitalfields was the scene of a series of brutal murders, the police failed to detect the assassin . . . the inhabitants formed them-selves into 'vigilance associations' and undertook nightly the patrol of the streets.*

But while the public were scared and angry, they were also morbidly fascinated by the most intimate details of the vile events. Even as the murders were taking place, a shop on the Whitechapel Road was displaying a Jack the Ripper waxwork show, and, according to the *East London Advertiser*, hundreds of people were prepared to pay a penny a time to stand in the upstairs of a house in Hanbury Street for the chance to gawp down into the yard where Annie Chapman's body had been found.

As the killings continued and rumours abounded, there were calls for any suspects who were apprehended to be lynched, to put an end to it once and for all. But who were these suspects?

Some of them were unfortunate lunatics whose appearance just happened to fit with the public's image of the crazed monster who surely had to be responsible, while others were accused simply because they were foreign – most often also Jewish – because how could a sane Englishman have committed such hideous crimes?

There were, and continue to be, theories suggesting far more high-profile suspects, including Prince Albert Victor – the same Prince 'Eddy' who was implicated in the Cleveland Street homosexual brothel scandal; the author of *Alice's Adventures* in *Wonderland*, Lewis Carroll; the artist Walter Sickert, who has been famously 'championed' by the crime writer Patricia Cornwell; and even Dr Barnardo and the Prince of Wales, Eddy's father.

One of the more bizarre names thrown into the pot was that of Frederick Charrington, who was well known for rejecting the work of his brewing family, even though the easy life and all the great financial rewards would have been his one day He had done so as a result of witnessing a man brutalizing his starving wife and children as they begged him for money for food; the man had been trying to enter a Bethnal Green pub owned by the Charrington family at the time. Frederick Charrington's reaction was to turn his life upside-down and take up philanthropic work on a major scale. But this did not leave his character unsullied.

While those who have speculated about his involvement have not gone so far as to claim that Charrington was the actual murderer, the suggestion is that he was responsible for having the murders arranged. One theory goes that he wasn't just a good man who wanted to work as a temperance and anti-vice campaigner, he was a man revolted by the immoral way of life led by the poor that he witnessed in the East End. They lived so close to his comfortable home in Bow and to the family's brewery business in Whitechapel that he could not ignore them. He determined to rid the area of such people and set about having the women picked off one by one in an insane but righteous rage, believing that the rest would be driven away, terrified that they might be next.

Another theory is that he was responsible for the killings being carried out, but for rather less misguidedly 'moral' reasons. This time the argument goes that he was masquerading as a 'good man', but was really taking advantage of legislation that enabled people to report case houses – the brothels – which would then be closed down and a reward given to the person doing the reporting. More importantly, if they had the means, that person could then buy the vacated premises. But the girls weren't so easily persuaded away from their regular stamping grounds. The contention is that Frederick Charrington wanted the properties –

London's population was growing at a rate of knots, housing stock was at a premium and potentially there was a lot of money to be made – and the murders were a means of scaring the women away. After all, who wanted to live in a place where there were 'brides' hanging around your doorstep?

Maybe not the most likely of theories, but as likely as some others, including the demented midwife theory told to me by my late grandmother, whose own mother had worked in the music halls at the time and had passed on the notion to her. Or the royal conspiracy idea, which involves a complicated story about an illegitimate baby being fathered by the most probably homosexual Prince Eddy, ritualistic Masonic slaughter, the upper echelons of the medical profession and generally rather a lot of wild-eyed over-excited conjecture. This all resulted from a half-baked television programme, which led to the publication of one of the most widely read books on the murders ever written, *Jack the Ripper: The Final Solution* by Stephen Knight.

Some other suspects who have been mooted in perhaps a more thought-out way include Dr Cream, the convicted murderer we met earlier, James Maybrick, Joseph Barnett, Aaron Kosminski, Montague John Druitt, George Chapman, Dr Francis Tumblety, Michael Ostrog and John Pizer, otherwise known as 'Leather Apron'. The favourites were once narrowed down to Montague Druitt, George Chapman and James Maybrick, but now it is the more recently discovered Tumblety who is being most seriously considered.

This quack doctor, who kept a collection of pickled wombs, used many aliases, was accused of frequent incidents of violence and was living in the right place at the right times. He is, according to serious students of the crimes, included in the elite circle of what they consider to be the only possible suspects – Tumblety, Ostrog, Druitt and Kosminski. These four, according to the Metropolitan Police, were also the four favoured by the police officers working on the case at the time of the murders.

But of course this list of suspects includes only those people who actually came under any sort of suspicion. If the killer had been able to blend in with his surroundings because of his apparent 'normality', as modern psychologists would suggest, then perhaps it should come as no surprise that he was never found in the maze of alleyways and courts of the Victorian East End.

As the murders were provoking fear, prurient interest and possibly copy-cat attacks, they were also, like more recent 'Ripper' murders in Yorkshire and Cambridge, for example, generating a rash of hoax letters, which were received by the police, the press and the Vigilance Committee. Purportedly coming from the killer, they added considerably to the myths surrounding the case. Even the murderer's sobriquet – Jack the Ripper – still held by many to be genuine, came from the infamous 'Dear Boss' letter, which, even though police at the time quickly dismissed as being a deception, had soon lodged itself firmly in the popular imagination as being real. The view now is that it was probably written by a journalist eager for a scoop and anxious to maintain the high levels of sales that the reports on the killings were generating throughout the press both at home and abroad.

Literally hundreds of fraudulent letters were sent, and there was also the legendary chalked message found on the wall of the buildings in Goulston Street that is spelt and transcribed in various ways, but is believed to have read: 'The Juwes are the men that will not be blamed for nothing'. But with only a handful of perpetrators being charged, investigators into the history of the murders have clung to the idea that at least some of the letters must be authentic. The most popular contender for being a genuine piece of correspondence coming from the killer's hand is that received by George Lusk, the leader of the Whitechapel Vigilance Committee. This communication came accompanied by a piece of kidney, and as one of the victims, Catherine Eddowes, had recently been found with a kidney missing, it added support to the belief that it was real. Cynics, however, suggest that it was a joke perpetrated by a mischievous medical student.

Whatever the theories regarding victims, suspects and correspondents – even the one claiming to be 'from Hell' – the events surrounding the Ripper murders certainly gained Whitechapel a worse reputation than it already deservedly had. In May 1901, when Elizabeth Austin was murdered by cutting and stabbing, it was widely reported that the crime had been committed in Whitechapel, when it had actually occurred in a common lodging house in Dorset Street, Spitalfields. In the Victorian version of today's MPs fretting about bad news causing so-called 'white flight' from their inner-city constituencies, the vicar of St Jude's wrote in complaint to *The Times*:

> *I advance this little protest because . . . it would appear that in past years murders done anywhere 'down east' or even within the august area of the City itself [Mitre Square, where Catherine Eddowes died, is in the City of London] have been too hastily attributed to Whitechapel, causing . . . great detriment hereabouts and the consequent departure of many well-known residents whose absence could ill be spared to less notorious neighbourhoods. Of the state of things which makes this murder possible, and the discovery of the murder impossible, I will not presume to say anything except that many of us feel that these things will continue to be as long as public opinion seems to assume it to be inevitable that parts of the 'East-end' should have a smaller proportion of police and a larger amount of lawlessness than should be looked for, let us say, in South Kensington.*

It is also interesting to note that the lodgings where the murder occurred, along with several others in Dorset Street, Whites Row and Little Paternoster Row – all of them notoriously run-down, unsavoury areas – were owned by Mr William Crossingham, a man who, like many of his fellow landlords, employed others to do the dirty work of running them, while they lived somewhere far more pleasant, in his case in Western Road, Romford, then a pleasantly leafy, market town.

A link that is not often mentioned in relation to the Whitechapel murders concerns the Tower of London. Martha Tabram, a.k.a. Emma or Martha Turner, the woman considered by some to be one of the early victims of Jack, was believed to have been killed with a bayonet, and so the culprit was sought among the soldiers garrisoned in the area. As can be seen from the pitiful lists of the possessions found on the bodies of women like Martha, they had little choice but to live from hand to mouth. Martha tried to earn money legally by hawking cheap trinkets of the type supplied by the swag shops, but she couldn't survive on her meagre earnings, so bolstered her wages by selling herself on the streets of Spitalfields and Whitechapel.

Like many other women in the Victorian sex trade, Martha spent a large proportion of her earnings on drink, just as prostitutes in the area today, according to the reports of the charities working with the women, spend most of their earnings on drink and drugs. Choosing to block out a reality too vile to cope with is perhaps not surprising, and so Martha and her friends would go off on regular benders.

On 6 August 1888, a Bank Holiday Monday, Martha and Mary Ann Connelly, better known as 'Pearly Poll', were seen in the company of a couple of soldiers – identified by some as guardsmen – on an extended pub crawl in and around Whitechapel. Close to midnight, the women separated, going off with their respective soldiers – Poll to Angel Alley and Martha to George Yard, presumably to do a bit of business and to earn the money for a bed for the night. In the early hours, a resident of George Yard Buildings saw someone huddled on the stairs and thought little of it, taking the person to be one of the many homeless who were forced to take shelter wherever they could. It wasn't unusual to come across someone who, without the few pennies needed to pay for a bed in one of the common lodging houses, had crept into a tenement stairwell, where they could at least be away from the worst of the bad weather and the dangers of the street. But just before five on the morning of the 7th, in the growing daylight, another resident, John Reeves, was leaving the buildings and realized that what his neighbour had wrongly supposed to be a homeless person sleeping rough was in fact a body surrounded by a pool of blood. Martha had been stabbed thirty-nine times. The inquest concluded that she had been attacked with a dagger and a bayonet, and it was deduced, therefore, that a member of the military would be the most likely suspect.

On Thursday 9 August Pearly Poll came forward to identify the victim and she agreed to try to identify the man she believed to be the culprit. From her first descriptions, it appeared that he was a member of the Tower Garrison. On the 13th, when Poll was again located by the authorities – after going missing, probably on another one of her benders – the men were paraded on the Broad Walk within the Tower for her to inspect. Despite taking what has been reported as up to two hours to scrutinize the men, Poll wasn't much help. All she could come up with was (according to different versions) either 'They had white bands round their hats', thus identifying them as being from another regiment, who were then lined up in their own barracks at a later date, when attempts at identification also failed; or that although she couldn't see the men with whom she and Martha had spent that particular evening, she thought that at least half of them had been customers of hers on previous occasions. Neither of her comments proved to be helpful in the investigations.

One contemporary idea was that the Whitechapel murders came to a halt because the killer had left the country, but that his blood lust hadn't been slaked. In February 1889, the *Penny Illustrated Paper* published the following piece, which starts off reasonably but ends up looking like nothing more than another attempt to cash in on the interest that was still surrounding the case, and that continues to do so:

It would seem that 'Jack the Ripper' has transferred himself from the Old World to the New, and is practising his horrible crimes with as much impunity in the Far West as he did in the east of London. Sometime ago it was reported that some unknown criminal had perpetrated several murders of the well known Whitechapel type upon the outcast women in Jamaica. A similar outbreak has occurred in Nicaragua. The last Whitechapel murder was committed on Lord

Mayors Day, November 9th, since which time there have been no similar atrocities in the east of London. We now learn that at the beginning of January similar atrocities were taking place in Nicaragua, and that about the end of December equally barbarous mutilations are reported from Jamaica. It would be interesting to know whether any steamer left the Thames after November 9th, and after calling at Jamaica in December proceeded to Central America. If such a steamer exists there seems a strong possibility that the murderer will be found among her crew – at any rate, the clue is one which might well be followed up by our detectives.

In addition to all these theories about the numbers of victims, possible suspects, conspiracies – royal and otherwise – arcane rituals and the persistence of the crimes, there is another very Victorian aspect that has been attributed to the case. This is the notion that the solution to these puzzling crimes *was* actually arrived at. Not surprisingly, considering all the other weird attributes ascribed to the case, it was believed that this solution was achieved by the force of psychic powers.

The name put forward as the supernatural investigator who assisted the police in nailing the killer and finally making the arrest was Robert James Lees. Lees was supposed to have been haunted by visions of terrible murders – murders which then actually occurred. He took his story to the police on several occasions and was at first dismissed as being a crank, but once he offered more material evidence he was finally taken seriously. When Lees went on to show the police the house where the man he named as the murderer was living, the crazed suspect was arrested and secreted away in a lunatic asylum.

The problem with this theory is that the Whitechapel murders occurred seven years before the stories about Robert James Lees first began to appear in newspapers – the first of them was printed in the Chicago press in 1895 – and the facts presented there bear little resemblance to those that are generally accepted to hold water (and even some of those increasingly look rather leaky). It is most likely that the link between the celebrated unsolved murders and any incidence of psychic phenomena simply made for a good story, a guaranteed best-seller to a suggestible Victorian readership eager for yet more sensation. For, as we shall see, psychic phenomena had become something of a nineteenth-century rage.

7

CON MEN, TRICKSTERS, CLAIRVOYANTS AND FRAUDS

Tricks on Greenhorns: These are too numerous to mention, for they comprise all the snares that human ingenuity can set for credulity. To avoid them there is but one maxim - be on your guard.

Charles Dickens Jnr, *Dictionary of London*, 1879

There is no one so gullible as an ordinary member of the British public. He will invest his last penny in an undertaking of which he knows absolutely nothing, although if he reads his newspaper, he must be perfectly well aware that kindred enterprises have, times without number, been exposed as out-and-out swindles.

Montagu Williams, *Round London. Down East and Up West*, 1894

*

Robert James Lees was the man acknowledged – by those who wished to believe in him – as the psychic investigator who solved the Jack the Ripper case. But he has also been dismissed by others – including both cynics and the police – as a crank, a con man and an attention seeker. We have to remember, however, that the time was then right for such individuals to prosper – if they put on a good enough show.

The burgeoning interest in anything to do with the occult was happening alongside the already established craze for mesmerism – the art of putting subjects into a trance by the use of 'animal magnetism', and once they were under the influence all sorts of inexplicable things could take place, from regaining sight to undergoing operations. As usual, *Punch* was more sceptical about the effects of putting on the 'fluence':

> *It was reported to the associated Association for the Encouragement of Mesmeric Mummery, that Dr Collyer had thrown a woman into such a state that a tooth was extracted from her head without her knowing anything about it. Professor Quizemall immediately brought under the notice of the meeting the following case that had occurred under his own eye as late as yesterday.*
>
> *The professor had observed an individual emerge from a public-house, who was evidently under a strong mesmeric influence. He oscillated considerably from side to side, and described various semi-circles, his arms and legs forming as it were radii, of which his body appeared to be the Centre. He at length fell with great violence on*

the pavement, and did not appear to suffer in the least, when a policeman began to manipulate upon his collar, and made a few passes with a thick staff over the shins of the patient, with the view most probably of disengaging the mesmeric matter. The patient struggled a good deal, and the professor might mention as a parallel case to that of Dr Collyer and the tooth, that the mesmerised individual lost the whole of one skirt of his coat without exhibiting any consciousness of the fact having happened.

A member wished to know how the case terminated. Professor Quizemall had seen the patient the next day, when he was completely dis-mesmerised, and was fully conscious of the loss of five shillings, taken from him no doubt by way of experiment though when under the mesmeric influence he had lost several sovereigns without being in the least aware of it.

Despite *Punch*'s mockery, when Mrs Hayden and Mrs Roberts arrived from America, bringing with them their new-fangled, New World spiritualism, Victoria's Britain was ripe for the taking. It didn't take long for table-rapping and table-turning to become a private and public fad here in the Old World. The mediums were soon filling every available space, from the front parlours of the well-heeled to large theatres, catering for the hordes of enthusiastic fans of the new sensation, all of whom were eager to experience the spirits answering their questions by means of coded raps and tilts and turns of the table. And this was still happening despite the fact that one of the famous Fox sisters, who had started the whole ball rolling in America in the 1840s, had stated quite plainly that the whole thing had been an act, just trickery and nonsense, and that every demonstration, whether in America or London, had been nothing more than a con. The rapping noises had been made by their knee and toe joints clicking – just as three medical investigators had argued all along. There were even newspaper advertisements for do-it-yourself medium para-phernalia, available from J. Theobald and Co. of Church Street, Kensington:

Spirit Rapping
Every Person a Medium
Full and Complete Apparatus for Spirit Rapping &c,
comprising
Rapper Battery, Wires, Contact Keys, Springs, Connections,
Wires &c.
Complete. Carriage-free 5s. 6d., with Full Instructions.

*

Yet people wanted to believe, all sorts of people, and in his book *The Table-Rappers*, Ronald Pearsall gives evidence of the Queen and Prince Albert, the royal couple themselves, having a keen interest in the craze for table-turning, clair-voyance and other psychic phenomena.

A demand for ever more thrilling experiences was growing and very quickly sitting in the circle at a full-blown seance had become all the rage, with spirit instruments playing, ghostly hands and feet appearing, and fully formed spirits materializing before the excited sitters. Conditions in the seances were carefully controlled, with the low lighting adding to the otherworldly atmosphere and, more importantly, providing cover for the people orchestrating the circle as they slipped prosthetic hands or feet over their own feet and then raised their legs and waved them over the table top without their deception being detected. *The spirits are amongst us!*

Coins could be picked up with naked toes and dropped into glass tumblers, so the sitters experienced both a materialization and a clattering sound to astonish them. Spirit writing and numbers would appear on slates – blank ones being swapped by sleight of hand for ones that had already been written on – with the appropriate question having been noted and suitable answers having been palmed to give the correct response to the psychic's enquiries. Phosphorescent paint would give a suitably otherworldly glow to the spirit emerging from a seance cabinet. *Again the circle is blessed! This time with an actual visitation!*

The ever-increasing fervour for such demonstrations meant that opportunities to exploit the grieving, the credulous and those merely seeking sensation abounded, and the world of the spirits became ever more – commercially – competitive. Mediums worked hard and sometimes dirtily to expose their rivals as shams, as did stage magicians, and learned societies were set up to expose the whole lot of them as confidence tricksters.

Two conjurors praised in the *Penny Illustrated Paper* for

their efforts to expose the sham – albeit in an entertaining and profitable way – were Maskelyne and Cooke. The climax to their show is described:

Mr Maskelyne is a determined foe to the spiritualists; and he selects for exposure one of the latest 'mediums' who have performed before the London public: the fair-haired Mrs Fay, whose puerile tricks are done by Mr Cooke with a celerity no 'spiritualist' could excel. There's the old familiar cabinet a la Davenport brothers [celebrated 'spiritualists' from the United States] with this difference: it is put together before the spectators, who are represented on the stage by two gentlemen who have volunteered to try their best to see how the illusions are managed. Mr Cooke, his limbs bound fast by cords, is seated on a camp stool and tied fast to rings at the back of the cabinet. The regulation curtain is dropped, and in less than a minute, tambourines are played inside the cabinet, and other so-called spiritualist phenomena occur. The curtain is then drawn up by Mr Maskelyne – who keeps up a running fire of satire against spiritualism and all its works – and Mr Cooke is seen quietly seated and bound as before . . . It is the dark seance which most astonishes the audience. Whilst Mr Cooke is still kept a prisoner in the cabinet the gas is turned out, and the hall is in complete darkness for a minute or so. During this time tambourines and banjos, dimly lit by phosphorescent light that throws a halo round them, float over the heads of the spectators, faintly strumming and beating all the while, and finally fall with a clang on the stage. In another instant the hall is light, and it is impossible to detect the agency by which the banjos and tambourines were circulated in mid-air. As tangible tokens of the dark seance, flowers are discovered in the laps of some of the perplexed visitors; and one of the most agreeable entertainments in town is brought to a close by the assurance that Mr Maskelyne is no 'spiritualist' as 'spiritualists' have averred, but an honest and hearty hater and exposer of the humbug by which so many people have been deceived.

With skills such as those of Maskelyne and Cooke, it wasn't usually that difficult to expose such trickery, but there was one man who defied all efforts. That man was D. D. Home.

Home was an individual who put on some spectacular displays which defied even the most conscientious of sceptical Victorian investigators, but he was also a man who was happy to relieve a wealthy widow of her inheritance – purportedly on the instruction of her dead husband. When people who had witnessed some of Home's more inexplicable phenomena – including feats such as levitation and, most spectacularly, floating in and out of third-floor windows – were questioned it is interesting that, as with most observers of these things, there were disagreements among the observers. They couldn't agree on what had actually been seen, or about the timings and the order in which the events had taken place. But those disposed to have faith can, as ever, convince themselves of many things, and will continue to take the knowing high ground against cynics and sceptics.

In the 1870s, Henry Slade, another spiritualist medium, was also wowing London, this time with his slate writings, claiming to be able to channel messages from his dead wife.

He was building himself quite a reputation, and a very good income, until Edwin Lankester, an evolutionary biologist colleague of Charles Darwin, decided to investigate his claims. Like the other well-to-do attendees of his circles, Lankester paid to sit at one of Slade's seances and was duly shown the blank slate on which the spirit message would mystically appear. But before Slade had even begun communing with the spirit world, Lankester grabbed the slate from his hands, showing that written on it was the answer to a question not yet asked. Slade was arrested, convicted but released on a legal technicality. He fled the country and resumed his business abroad. A disappointment for those who had hoped for so much more, for those who had wanted to believe.

Maybe more surprisingly, the hard-nosed journalist W. T. Stead had a strong interest in psychic matters, going so far as to set up and edit *Borderland*, a paper devoted to the subject. Stead was also an associate of Madame Blavatsky. But he wasn't the only radical campaigner who became involved with her. Blavatsky was a woman whose Theosophical Society continues to be questioned regarding its validity and purported aims to this day, yet the radical Annie Besant went so far as to become not only a convert to Theosophy – Blavatsky's religious philosophy, known as 'divine wisdom' – but one of its leaders.

When Helena Petrovna Blavatsky's marriage broke down, she decided to leave Russia and travel to the East. She reappeared ten years later as *Madame* Blavatsky, a psychic medium with some extraordinary tales to tell of her findings and experiences while she was living abroad. By the time she had established herself in America in the 1870s, she was no longer a run-of-the-mill spiritualist but had brought in some fine added value. She now spoke authoritatively about various bits of mysticism and ideas regarding reincarnation that she had garnered from an assortment of religions and belief systems – everything from Hinduism to the Kabbalah – selected pieces of their theories and mangled philosophies all thrown into her one big numinous pot.

In 1875, Blavatsky and a Colonel Olcott went 'legit' and co-founded the Theosophical Society in New York, moving their base to Adyar in India three years later. The society taught that a group of so-called Mahatmas existed in Tibet with powers far superior to those of ordinary humans. These beings could work all sorts of miracles for their Theosophist friends – ranging from something that sounds just like that old favourite, spirit writing, to moving solid objects, apparently without human agency – and other phenomena that were very similar to those occurring during less exotic spiritualist seances.

Many controversial claims and counter-claims were made for the truth or otherwise of these alleged marvels, including assertions that Blavatsky had openly admitted that she used deception in a series of letters that ex-members of the society had forwarded to an Indian journal, which the editor had then gone on to publish.

The British Society for Psychical Research became interested in all the rumours and sent Richard Hodgson, an experienced investigator from St Johns College, Cambridge, to report on what was happening in India. Hodgson condemned the phenomena as fraudulent, saying that they were produced by simple sleight of hand and mechanical trickery, using props such as trap doors and mirrors that would have been familiar to even the most unskilled of cheap stage conjurors. Hodgson further added that any supporters of Blavatsky who maintained that they had observed the events personally were nothing more than self-deluded. Basically, those people had done what believers in Home's powers had done – they had seen what they wanted to, and, having such a strong desire to believe, they had been perfect targets for persuasion that all sorts of things had occurred before their very eyes.

Madame Blavatsky felt the need to move on again, this time to London, where she was to meet and convert Annie Besant, a woman who had previously rejected religious belief and had been a member of the National Secular Society and of the socialist Fabians. When Madame Blavatsky died in 1891, Annie became joint 'Outer head of the esoteric section' of the Theosophical Society. She settled in India, where she studied and, radical that she continued to be, campaigned for Indian Home Rule.

Strangely, the 'organ of Theosophy' figures in the work of a nineteenth-century Viennese doctor called Franz-Joseph Gall, who was responsible for introducing another strange belief to the world: phrenology. Gall believed that the brain contained twenty-seven organs, each of which was related to a specific human function – with the organ of Theosophy being linked to a person's sense of religious belief. The organs covered every other function from parental love to the impulse to murder and to steal. Gall's belief was that, depending on how often they were used, the organs grew or shrivelled accordingly. The effect of this was to cause the famous 'bumps' on the head that could then be examined by the skilled practitioner, who would literally read the character according to the shape of the skull. The procedure came into its own in Victorian Britain, the almost perfect environment for such a belief to flourish, and then, to an even greater extent, it took off in America. Not everyone across the Atlantic was so taken with it; Ambrose Bierce, in his *Devil's Dictionary*, described it as a means of picking the pocket through the scalp, and it did provide plenty of opportunities for conning trusting members of the public. There was even a craze for postal phrenology, with the head being 'read' from photographs and hair samples, much like the laboratories today that will supply a list of allergies from hair samples sent to them in the mail. Phrenology has now been widely dismissed, although it is acknowledged that Gall was correct in his belief that human function and behaviour are located in various parts of the brain.

With no national health service available, a quick visit to the doctor costing more than many could afford and the state of medical knowledge and medicines being crude and ineffective when compared to those available today, it is no wonder that alternatives such as phrenology were sought. Similarly, snake oil salesmen with their 'remedies' could make a tidy profit, despite their pills, potions and lotions either being useless or, worse, containing positively dangerous substances.

Between 1876 and 1877 the photographer John Thomson collaborated with Adolphe Smith to create an illustrated record of day-to-day living conditions among the London poor. The following description of a street vendor of quack remedies comes from their *Street Life in London*:

> . . . *togged like a military swell [he] scares the people into buying his pills. He has half-a-dozen bottles filled with different fluids he works with, turning one into the other. He turns a clear fluid black, and says, 'Ladies and gentlemen, this is what happens to your blood when exposed to the fogs of London. "Without blood there is no life!" You seem bloodless, my friends; look at each other.' They look, and almost believe him. 'Next to no blood is impure blood! This is your condition, I can describe your symptoms; I offer you the only safe, certain, and infallible remedy.' This style of 'patter' makes the pills fly . . .*

The silver-tongued salesmen also provided free street entertainment and lunch-time crowds from the nearby City – described to Raphael Samuel by Arthur Harding as the 'white collar brigade' – would gather around the quacks' pitches in Shoreditch to listen to their intriguing patter and have a bit of a laugh, much as their contemporary counterparts today flock to the lap-dancing 'gentlemen's clubs', seeking entertainment in those same shady areas on the boundaries of the City.

Photography was employed in less scrupulous ways than that used by Thomson in his recording of London life, to assist confidence tricksters in separating mugs from their money. Bereaved individuals, eager to believe in an afterlife, had their photographs taken by psychics who would then produce miraculous spirit photographs showing not only the living sitter, but also images of their dearly departed floating around them. Crooks will always find a way of using new technology to exploit the public, especially those who are vulnerable.

One type of con that didn't seem to arouse much opposition or anger – so long as it provided sufficient amusement for the punters – was the travelling fair or peep show, which, in the words of the great showman 'Lord' George Sanger, showed such exotica as the 'Hottentot Venus, drawfs, Miss Scott the Two-Headed Lady, Yorkshire Jack the Living Skeleton, and learned pigs and fortune-telling ponies galore'.

Before we allow ourselves to be contemptuous of such immature interest in the different and the bizarre, it is worth thinking about the coverage in our contemporary press of events such as the separating of conjoined twins – complete with photographs and diagrams – or incidences of images of Jesus appearing on a slice of aubergine or in a grease smear on a paper napkin. And while educated ponies able to tell fortunes might have been accepted as no more than a bit of fun, they were still popular in my childhood in the 1950s, when I witnessed the skills of Tony the Wonder Horse in a variety show at the Hackney Empire. But fortune-telling by humans was seen by the Victorian authorities as a serious offence. One middle-aged woman in Mile End, for instance, who charged sixpence for each psychic reading, was sentenced to a month's hard labour after being caught with packs of cards and some arcane instructions regarding clairvoyance that had been ripped from a book. If you weren't caught, however, a reasonable wage could be made from foretelling the future. In the travelling fairs, if women used gimmicks in their routines, they could do even better. Budgerigars, which had first been introduced into Britain in 1840, were a popular attention-grabber, with the little green birds selecting cards with their beaks for the psychic to 'read' and then reassure the worried customers, who only wanted to hear that their troubles would soon be at an end and, in no time at all, good fortune would be smiling on them. With even todays 'serious' Sunday newspapers having their advisory and consoling horoscopes for the 'worried well', it can be imagined how popular any comforting guidance would have been for the truly worried.

One of the biggest gatherings of travelling fairs happened in Hyde Park to celebrate the coronation of Queen Victoria. The celebrations lasted for nine days and were graced with one of the era's most celebrated exhibits: Madame Stevens the pig-faced lady. The unfortunate-looking woman was actually a shaven-faced brown bear decked out in a bonnet, frock, shawl and gloves. The creature was strapped into a chair behind a cloth-draped table, under which was hidden a small boy. The showman asked questions to which Madame Stevens replied with appropriately pig-like grunts – prompted by the small boy poking the poor thing with a sharp stick. The showman explained her strange, animal-like speech to the audience: 'As you see, ladies and gentlemen, the young lady understands what is said perfectly, though the peculiar formation of her jaws has deprived her of the power of uttering human speech in return.' Madame Stevens's obviously contemptuous response when asked about her views on men was particularly appreciated by the audience.

Another favourite was Sanger's famous Pipe-smoking Tame Oyster, an illusion created by first offering the audience a live mollusc for them to examine, which the showman then palmed for a rigged-up oyster shell connected to rubber tubing hidden in the folds of the cloth on yet another of Sanger's conveniently draped tables. When Sanger popped the pipe in between the oyster's 'lips' it puffed away like a train – ably assisted by the small boy crouching under the table, without whom so many stunts could never have succeeded. It appears that there was no problem with the child smoking.

In his study of *London Labour and the London Poor*, Henry Mayhew describes less entertaining 'cons':

> *. . . beggars, are not 'lurkers' – a lurker being strictly one who loiters about for some dishonest purpose. Many modes of thieving as well as begging are termed 'lurking' – the 'dead lurk,' for instance, is the expressive slang phrase for the art of entering dwelling-houses during divine service. The term 'lurk,' however, is mostly applied to the several modes of plundering by representations of sham distress.*

'Sham distress' being the key words here: a condition that will be familiar to anyone today who has come across con artists working in the tradition of Victorian false begging-letter writers and cadgers. The man or woman at the railway station who – unluckily – seems to be the victim of robbery just about every day of the week and only needs a couple of quid to get home, or the scooter owner who approached me as I sat in my car near the Rotherhithe Tunnel waiting for a red light to change. The poor chap had just run out of petrol and needed a few measly litres of fuel to get him home, could I help? I probably would have slipped him a fiver had I not seen him parking the bike and approaching motorists at the lights in exactly the same place and manner the day before.

Mayhew disapproved of such scams, both those that depended on the trustful nature of the mark targeted by the con man and those in which rules or laws were flouted in a way that would benefit the perpetrator:

> *It is of these alone that I propose here treating – or rather of that portion of them which pretends to deal in manufactured articles. In*

a few instances the street-sellers of small articles of utility are also the manufacturers. Many, however, say they are the producers of the things they offer for sale, thinking thus to evade the necessity of having a hawkers licence. The majority of these petty dealers know little of the manufacture of the goods they vend, being mere tradesmen. Some few profess to be the makers of their commodities, solely with the view of enlisting sympathy, and thus either selling the trifles they carry at an enormous profit, or else of obtaining alms.

It is also the shoddiness of the merchandise that Mayhew objected to, especially as they were often being sold to those who could not afford to pay the full shop price for the items and believed that they were getting a genuine bargain:

An inmate of one of the low lodging-houses has supplied me with the following statement . . . 'the great branch of trade among these worthies, was the sale of sewing cotton, either in skeins or on reels. In the former case, the article cost the "lurkers" about 8d. per pound; one pound would produce thirty skeins, which, sold at one penny each, or two for three halfpence, produced a heavy profit. The lurkers could mostly dispose of three pounds per day; the article was, of course, damaged, rotten, and worthless . . . ' Cotton on reels was – except to the purchaser – a still better speculation; the reels were large, handsomely mounted, and displayed in bold relief such inscriptions as the following: PIKE'S PATENT COTTON. 120 Yards. The reader, however, must divide the '120 yards,' here mentioned, by 12, and then he will arrive at something like the true secret as to the quantity; for the surface only was covered by the thread.

A more ambitious, and more profitable, scam was 'horse-making', the Victorian equivalent of the motor trade's illicit 'cut and shut' scam, in which two damaged vehicles are welded together to produce a 'new' car. This temporary beautifying and making youthful of old nags, usually purchased from the knacker man, is described as follows by Charles Manby Smith in his *Curiosities of London Life*:

> *There is hardly a disorder horse flesh is heir to the symptoms of which he cannot banish, by means of drug, knife, cautery or secret nostrum . . . By dint of shears, singeing, currycomb and brush . . . by the cunning application of ginger or cayenne to the jaws, the nostrils, the ears, or elsewhere, the dullest, worn out hack is stimulated in to sprightliness and demonstrations of blood and breeding.*

It wasn't only living horse flesh that could be used to earn a dishonest shilling or two. Diseased animals, which had been condemned as being unfit for human consumption, were slaughtered and sold to the poor, no questions being asked at such a knock-down price. Other bad foodstuffs were sold to the very poorest, who had no choice about where they shopped, usually daily, as they were living hand to mouth – as can be seen from the pitifully small amounts of tea and so on found on the prostitute victims of the Whitechapel murderer. There were also those who knowingly bought bad food – for example, from the cat's meat man, though they had no intention of feeding it to the cat. Then there was the deliberate adulteration of food by dodgy retailers, who would regularly add bulking agents. Milk, for instance, would have ground chalk diluted in water stirred in, and phoney weights could do a similar job for solid foodstuffs, conning the customer that they were buying more than they actually were. James Greenwood loathed both the practice and its practitioners, seeing it for what it was: nothing more than robbery of those who could least afford it.

You don't call it 'making,' you robbers of the counter and money-till, that is a vulgar expression used by 'professional' thieves; you allude to it as 'cutting it fine.' Neither do you actually plate copper pennies and pass them off on the unwary as silver half-crowns. Unless you were very hard driven indeed, you would scorn so low and dangerous a line of business. Yours is a much safer system of robbery. You simply palm off on the unwary customer burnt beans instead of coffee, and ground rice instead of arrowroot, and a mixture of lard and turmeric instead of butter. You poison the poor man's bread. He is a drunkard, and you are not even satisfied to delude him of his earnings for so long a time as he may happily live as a wallower in beer and gin, that is beer and gin as originally manufactured; you must, in order to screw a few halfpence extra and daily out of the poor wretch, put grains of paradise in his gin and cocculus indicus [a hallucinogenic] in his malt liquor! And, more insatiable than the leech, you are not content with cheating him to the extent of twenty-five per cent by means of abominable mixtures and adulteration, you must pass him through the mill, and cut him yet a little finer when he comes to scale! You must file your weights and dab lumps of grease under the beam, and steal an ounce or so out of his pound of bacon. If you did this after he left your premises, if you dared follow him outside, and stealthily inserting your hand into his pocket abstracted a rasher of the pound he had just bought of you, and he caught you at it, you would be quaking in the grasp of a policeman in a very short time, and branded in the newspapers as a paltry thief, you would never again dare loose the bar of your shop shutters. But by means of your dishonest scales and weights, you may go on stealing rashers from morning till night, from Monday morning till Saturday night that is, and live long to adorn your comfortable church pew on Sundays.

'Gin spinning', one of the types of adulteration mentioned by Greenwood, didn't seem to be a problem for the customers. This drink doctoring used additives including drugs, sweeteners and, most worryingly, water drawn straight from the Thames that apparently made the product more palatable for some consumers. The 'spun' product was variously known as 'Cordial Gin', 'OldTom' and 'Mountain Dew'. It was a highly profitable business: 'Three hogsheads of proof gin from the distillers shall in the course of a single night become transformed in to seven substantial hogsheads of "Cream of the Valley".'

Perhaps we fret more today about legal additives than illegal ones, but other types of 'spinning' certainly carry on. For example, the practice of producing 'cabbage' within the schmutter trade – the cheap end of the tailoring business – that has happened for as long as clothes have been mass-produced in places like the slop shops of Brick Lane.

This works by the skilful cutting of a bolt of cloth to produce enough 'spare' material to make extra garments, which are then sold 'informally' rather than going through the books, either by the boss with his knowledge or by his workers without.

There were more sophisticated scams that could bring even bigger profits. One such was auction-rigging – another swindle which is still in operation today. The manner varies, but the purpose was – and is – to control prices, keeping them unfairly, and illegally, low. The rigging ring might threaten potential buyers not to bid, or they might fix the auctioneer beforehand; they then decide which of the ring will bid for which lots, never bidding competitively against each other. The items bought would then be 'knocked out' between the gang in a later, real auction, held at a secret venue. The balance between the first price paid at the public auction and that which the member of the ring pays in the secret auction is divided up between them. If anyone did try to outbid the ring for their selected lots in the original sale, one of the gang would push the price ridiculously high and then, by prior arrangement with the auctioneer, would not actually pay for it but would return it for the next auction. That, of course, would only work if the auctioneer was as crooked as the gang – but, as always, a big enough bribe might turn the most supposedly honest of heads.

A more complex con was known as the established-business swindle. With increasing numbers of people coming to the capital to seek their fortunes, this worked particularly well in Victorian London. The set-up for the scam began with an advertisement placed in a newspaper, offering a business for sale – an example described by Charles Manby Smith relates to a housing agency. The individual – who is the mark for the con artists – turns up at the premises, eager to see the business concerned and to judge if it is worth the price being asked, but is immediately disappointed when told by the clerk that, unfortunately, there is already someone interested in buying it. The actual agent – the proprietor himself – then comes through from a back room and instructs the clerk to take the man's details. He adds that the would-be buyer – the mark – should return the day after tomorrow at a specified time as that is the deadline for his rival purchaser to come up with the asking price, and there is an outside chance that the rival will fail.

On his second visit, the mark's rival is already there and doesn't seem very happy. The clerk shows the mark through to the back room, clearly not wanting him to hear the exchange between his boss and the other man. But, of course, they make sure that he can hear every word. They are arguing, the agent insisting that the deadline is up and he cannot give the rival any longer to raise the funds to reach the full asking price. The man leaves. The agent brings his other prospective purchaser through from the back room and apologizes for any unpleasantness, then wonders if he is still interested in proceeding with an offer to purchase. He certainly is, particularly as he can see how busy the agency is. In the brief time since he has been brought through, the clerk has dealt with three new customers. He is more than ready to go ahead.

The agent shows him two years' worth of full accounts and, as a sign of goodwill, offers to let the would-be buyer spend a fortnight at the agency to see how it runs. The two weeks go very well, with the clerk showing him the ropes and new customers daily adding to the already healthy profits. The day comes for the buyer to take over his new business. He is at first surprised to see that the clerk hasn't turned up before him, as was his usual practice, but thinks there must be some simple explanation. He becomes more uncomfortable when not a single customer comes through the door, and, finally, by the end of the week it dawns on him that it has all been a means of swindling him out of his money – the agency never existed.

There were plenty of other far less complicated ways of parting a fool from his hard-earned cash, ones that depended purely on the greed of the mark.

A reasonably tidy but clearly poor young man would be walking through a respectable neighbourhood when he suddenly called out in surprise. What good fortune! He had found a ring! Right there, at his feet! As it happens, a well-dressed man is close by. He comes nearer and is curious to see what the lad has found. The young man expresses his delight. This ring must be worth at least five pounds; he'll get a good price for it at the pawnbroker's.

The older man is well aware that the finder has no clue as to the value of such a fine piece of jewellery and offers to cut out the middle man and give him the five pounds there and then. Not a bad return on a piece of junk that the young man has bought in large numbers, wholesale from a swag shop.

A simple scam that depended more on the gullibility of the mark than on greed involved a nasty form of blackmail, a crime at which the art dealer and collector Charles Howell became highly proficient. Howell moved in elevated artistic circles and would befriend and correspond with well-known Victorians including Ruskin, Whistler, Millais, the Rossettis and Swinburne. Howell's first move was to identify his victim's potentially embarrassing sexual predilection, which he would then feign to share; the poet Swinburne, for instance, was said to enjoy visiting homosexual brothels that catered for his specific sadomasochist tastes. Howell made sure that letters were exchanged between them, discussing his mark's preferences. When Howell had sufficient incriminating correspondence, the blackmail would begin. Howell would claim that he was so broke that he had had no choice but to pawn the collection, and, due to the eminence of the writer, it was worth a good deal. If the victim couldn't come up with enough funds to redeem the items, the pawnbroker was going to auction them off for what was sure to be a huge amount. The sensitivity of the material meant that Howell would make a tidy sum, but would lose a 'friend', which he did many times.

A less complex but still effective form of sexual blackmail was exposed in a letter to *The Times*:

A smartly dressed, well-looking boy comes up to you, and asks some frivolous question . . . He manages to keep you in conversation for some seconds, and walks on by your side as far into the obscurity as may be. On a sudden a man comes up, and asks, 'What are you doing with my son?' On this, the boy affects to cry, and hints that the gentlemen got into conversation with him for a grossly immoral purpose. The man then says, 'There, you hear what he says; now the only way to get out of it is to give the boy a sovereign, or to the police you go.' Now, Sir, a nervous man is so thrown off his guard by this threatened imputation, that he submits to this or any other infamous demand. Surely, Sir, the police must be remiss in their duty not to scare away a gang of monsters who loiter at dusk near what are meant to be 'public conveniences,' but which have become 'public nuisances.' The foregoing, Sir, happened to me the other night, and if you would insert the same, others might profit by my experience and loss.

As to whether the writer of the letter was telling the whole truth, it cannot be established, but he was lucky that he wasn't tricked into falling for a more elaborate version of this type of extortion – the so-called Badger Game. A married man with funds, or at least access to money, would be targeted. He would then be lured into a sexually compromising situation by the scam artist's accomplice – maybe a pretty woman, an attractive young man, a supposedly under-age child – or into some other socially unacceptable act – depending on which predilection had been identified by the criminals. The scam artist would then burst into the room at the 'right' moment, posing as the accomplice's husband or father. At a time when reputations and lives could be destroyed by scandal – probably one of the major differences between that era and our own – money would be demanded to hush up the unfortunate situation.

Perhaps the most pathetically deluded victims of a fraudster and blackmailer were those who fell prey to 'Madame Rachel' – as the widowed Sarah Rachel Leverson styled herself. Madame Rachel knew, just as manufacturers know today, that women are willing to pay fortunes for cosmetic preparations in the hope that they will work miracles. She set up shop in Bond Street and was soon doing good business, flogging her incredibly expensive, exotically named wares from her Temple of Beauty. But there was more to the emporium than a place where you could buy items that would, as the sign above the shop promised, keep you 'Beautiful for Ever'. In an adjoining premises, Madame Rachel opened the Arabian Baths, ostensibly a sort of Victorian spa where clients could choose from a range of therapies, but more importantly for her and her blackmailing ambitions, there were rooms that could be booked for illicit liaisons. Madame Rachel's range of services were soon providing her with a handsome income that she was raking in from the trusting, the desperate and the adulterous. It was to be the surprising actions of Mrs Borradaile, a frail-looking widow, that would finally put a stop to Madame Rachel's fraudulent games.

Mrs Borradaile began by purchasing potions and creams from the Temple of Beauty and then moved on to the treatments on offer in the Arabian Baths. While bathing, the unthinkable happened and a middle-aged man was able to catch a glimpse of her. Madame Rachel appeared and expressed her mortification to Mrs Borradaile that the gentleman concerned ,Lord Ranelagh, had been allowed to see her in the bath. But it wasn't all bad news . . . When he had seen the bathing woman, Lord Ranelagh had been so taken with her loveliness that he told Madame Rachel that he was determined they would marry. The only fly in the face cream, as it were, was the fact that Mrs Borradaile was a widow of a humble major in the Indian Army, while Ranelagh was an aristocrat and he would have to find a way of persuading his family of the suitability of the match. Until such time as he could do so, Madame Rachel told the widow, he would correspond with Mrs Borradaile, using Madame Rachel as their go-between. The letters duly arrived, and Mrs Borradaile was looking forward to a new life with a new husband – a man who thought her to be a great beauty. There was even icing on top of that cake: Lord Ranelagh was due to come in to a large inheritance. Unfortunately, until he did so, he was temporarily without means, being in dispute with his family – a terrible situation, whatever could be done about it? The widow fell for it, and within months Madame Rachel had bled her dry, leaving the woman with nothing. Madame Rachel thought that it didn't matter when Mrs Borradaile found out that there had been no interest in her, from Lord Ranelagh or anyone else, and that the letters were fraudulent and had actually been written by her. She believed that the widow would become such an object of derision if she tried to take the matter to court and her reputation would be ruined – factors which had so far protected the confidence trickster and blackmailer from being prosecuted on the evidence of her other victims. But Mrs Borradaile wasn't like the others, and despite her now almost comically cosmetically enhanced appearance, she took the matter to court. So it was that in 1868 Sarah Rachel Leverson was convicted for fraud and imprisoned. On her release she went straight back to her old ways, but she didn't have such a good run of luck this time. She was soon caught out, convicted and sent back to prison, where she died.

Requiring less organization and equipment than setting up Arabian Baths, card sharps and thimble riggers would travel around the country visiting race meetings. There, all they had to do was set up a little table and they were ready to take money from credulous punters with the three-card trick – also known as Chase the Lady – or having them believe that they could pick the correct one of the three thimbles under which the pea was concealed. Sometimes the thimble riggers would use halves of walnut shells instead of thimbles, or, as I remember from my childhood, the men working their pitches around Club Row would use little metal cups. A painting can be seen in Tate Britain, *The Derby Day* by William Powell Frith, dating from 1856-8, that shows a Victorian thimble rigger at work. It looks as if he is working solo, but the card sharps and riggers didn't operate alone. They acted in groups of up to six: the skilled man doing the actual sleight of hand, at least two keeping a lookout for the police, and up to three accomplices posing as members of the public. They would, of course, be allowed to win a few times, thus enticing genuine punters to try their own luck at such an easy way of making money.

The races were also a useful place for schneid or snide dropping – the passing off of false coins – as they could be palmed off when placing bets. If the coins were discovered by the bookie, the 'innocent' crook could simply claim that it was he who was the victim, as he had been given them earlier in payment for a win.

Another popular trick, which, like the three-card game, pulled in crowds of mugs convinced they could win, was the pieman scam. Pieman, otherwise known as Pitch and Toss, was a game in which two halfpennies or pennies were pitched on to a flat surface, usually a board placed on the floor, with the banker winning if the coins landed on the same face. To show honest intent, the coins would be supplied by the punter, but once the banker had palmed one of the coins for a double-header, the odds were greatly reduced – in his favour, of course.

So, as we can see, scams, cons, frauds and deception were rife in Victoria's supposedly good old days. But so too was dissent, and in the next chapter we will learn more of Annie Besant, whose radicalism probably had rather more impact on the lives of others than did her role in the Theosophy movement.

8

THE GOOD OLD DAYS, INDEED: DISSENT AND REVOLT

That this meeting [of the Fabian Society], being aware that the shareholders of Bryant and May are receiving a dividend of over 20 per cent, and at the same time are paying their workers only 2 ¼ d. per gross for making match-boxes, pledges itself not to use or purchase any matches made by this firm.

The Link, No. 21, 23 June 1888

[On] Monday a deputation from the parish of Bethnal Green waited upon MR PEEL to request that some measures might be devised to suppress the dreadful riots and outrages that take place every night in the parish, by a lawless gang of thieves, consisting of 5 or 600. The gang rendezvous in a brick-field at the top of Spicer-street, Spitalfields, and out-posts are stationed to give an alarm, should any of the civil power approach, their cry is

'Warhawk,' as a signal for retreat. On the brick kilns in this field they cook whatever meat and potatoes they plunder from the various shops in the neighbourhood, in the open day and in the face of the shopkeeper. Their outrages have been of the daring kind; there are now no less than five individuals lying in the London Infirmary, without hopes of recovery, that have fallen into the hands of the gang. Within the last fortnight, upwards of 50 persons have been robbed, and cruelly beaten, and one of the gang was seen one day last week to produce amongst some of his associates, nearly half-a-hat-full of watches. – MR PEEL gave immediate orders for a detachment of Horse Patrol to be stationed day and night in the neighbourhood; and on Friday morning a party of forty men, to be under the jurisdiction of the Magistrates of Worship-street Police-office, were mounted; they are a party of able-bodied men who have held situations in the army, accoutred with cutlasses, pistols, and blunderbusses. - They will be in constant communication with forty of the dismounted patrol.

press cutting from the Tower Hamlets local history archive, no source given

*

As the gulf between the Victorian rich and poor grew ever wider, so discontent mounted among those who felt that they were being left behind while others were prospering at their expense. The labouring classes were seen as fit to service the needs of the rich – from sweating on the factory floor to slaving at the scullery sink – but they were not considered fit to share in the prosperity. The bubbling up of dissatisfaction began to take concrete form in the establishment of movements determined to do something about the lack of fairness and representation. With political upheaval blazing across mainland Europe, the property-owning classes of Great Britain should have been trembling whenever a dip in the trade cycle was followed by a rise in unemployment. Or when harsh winters resulted in yet worse conditions having to be endured by the growing numbers of shabbily housed and, worse still, homeless people, they should have been waiting for the riots. Especially when the bad weather, which had traditionally caused disastrous harvests, made matters worse in the diminishing country-side, where food production and jobs were becoming more and more scarce with the rampant urbanization that was sweeping across the land. In the final thirty years of Victoria's reign these factors were to be exacerbated by increasing competition from abroad as other countries caught up in the race to industrialize and to mass-produce goods for export. Yet, despite the 'new journalism' produced by the likes of W. T. Stead – which was able to flourish following the abolition of newspaper taxes in the middle of the century – with its allegedly sensational exposes of the conditions in which the exploited classes were forced to live, the majority of the better-off still ignored the plight of the labouring poor. Some, like Charles Booth, refused to believe that the reporting could be true, and blamed do-gooding socialists who wanted to overstate the case to further their own political aims.

Booth, however, was not like most of the doubters. His reaction was to test the reports by launching a staggering, seventeen-volume social study, which was to be carried out by his meticulous fieldworkers. The results of their investigations would literally chart the East End in the form of a shocking poverty map. This huge project was conducted between 1886 and 1903. Booth's conclusion was that the enormity of the problem had actually been understated, and his efforts were a sad vindication of much of the work that had earlier been dismissed as mere sensational exaggeration. On the one hand, maybe we should be surprised that the response to this situation wasn't total anarchy or insurrection. But on the other, as we will see, there was more rebellion than might have been expected in what is still held by many to have been a golden age of gentility, deference and all-round good behaviour – with the rich man enjoying life in his castle and the poor man knowing his place well and truly at the gate.

Booth's work wasn't completed until two years after Queen Victoria's death, but during the time she was on the throne – almost at the beginning of her reign, in fact – even Her Majesty's army was rebelling. In 1838 three unnamed soldiers – a sergeant, a corporal and a rifleman, all members of the Rifle Brigade – were apprehended on board a ship as they tried to flee to America. The reason for their flight was that they had stolen the entire regiment's wages. After their capture, the three men were taken to the Tower of London and there they were held in custody in the Middle Tower, to await court-martial. However, six days later, and defying all the odds, they escaped from the confines of the massively fortified Tower by climbing out of a window. They then made their way along a ledge, managed to cross the moat and, after clambering up the retaining wall, made their way to Tower Hill – and so to freedom.

But it was the poorer classes rather than the reasonably paid and housed armed forces who were expected to exist in the slum conditions and who displayed the most signs of discontent. Adding to the brew of poverty and disaffection were the strains caused by waves of immigrants, such as those escaping famine in Ireland and, later, those coming from Eastern Europe, fleeing the pogroms of Tsarist Russia. Overcrowding and competition for work meant that there was even less chance that the conditions of the worst off in society would just sort themselves out. But it wasn't only this completely excluded group who were disaffected. It is ironic that the new technologies that were contributing to the wealth of (some of) the nation were being employed by disgruntled members of the slightly better-off but still unrepresented lower-middle and labouring classes to produce and distribute affordable literature to rally others in support of their causes. One such was a newspaper, the radical *Northern Star*, which played a vital role in politicizing and uniting the mass membership of the Chartist movement.

In 1832 the Reform Bill had allowed for an extension to the existing franchise, but it benefited few. Rather than doing away with the corrupt means of electing the country's representatives to Parliament, and introducing universal male suffrage, the lines were merely redrawn, Now the determining factor was who had property and who did not. The subsequent dissatisfaction would see the development and growth of a movement of lower-middle and educated working classes that would demand more say in how they were governed. Accompanied by sometimes violent demonstrations, strikes and pickets, petitions for the People's Charter were organized to show support for its six demands. These were as follows: voting by secret ballot to prevent any possibility of intimidation; the ending of the property qualification for Members of Parliament, so that a man of whatever means could stand; similarly, MPs should be paid; constituencies should be of equal size as a matter of fairness; parliamentary elections should take place yearly; and there should be universal adult male suffrage. Rights for women were not included in the Charter, but, as with the miners' strike of 1984 – 5, females played a prominent part in fighting for the rights of their menfolk. Paradoxically, the battle for votes for women would be won long after the end of the reign of Queen Victoria, the extraordinarily powerful monarch and first Empress of India.

When the People's Charter was drawn up in 1838, it had

the galvanizing effect of bringing together radical groups from around the country into a cohesive unit with one single aim: the granting of the six demands. However, this didn't mean that there weren't separate groups among them who saw the movement as an opportunity to press for more sweeping changes, such as general strikes and a People's Parliament, and, on the whole, these were also the people who were advocates of the use of violence in the campaign. In 1839 the leadership decided that they had enough signatures, totalling over one and a quarter million, to make Parliament listen to their demands. The Charter was duly presented – and promptly rejected.

The views of those who had supported the use of violence were now listened to more sympathetically, if not universally, among the membership, and rioting broke out around the country. In one incident, the Chartists marched on Newport and a gun battle ensued between them and the armed soldiers who were lying in wait. Twenty marchers were killed outright and others were fatally wounded, while many more received serious injuries. Arrests were made and convicted men hanged for treason. Rather than enraging the movement into collective action, the events in Wales were followed by disagreement and fragmentation. But Chartism as a countrywide force would continue, in no small measure due to the economic depression that has come to be known as the 'Hungry Forties', despite the fact that it lasted from 1837 to 1842. In 1842 workers were again striking and causing industrial unrest by sabotaging machinery in the so-called 'Plug Riots', where boilers were put out of action and factories made inoperable. Also in that year, there was the presentation of another, even bigger, petition to Parliament. This time there were over three million signatures; surely that many people couldn't be so easily ignored? They could. The petition was thrown out again.

Despite many more arrests and harsh sentences being doled out to agitators and campaigners, in 1848 a third attempt was made at submitting the wishes of the people in the form of a petition to Members of Parliament. It was significant that this was shaping up to be a year of revolution right across Europe, when the Chartists mustered at Kennington Common on 10 April 1848 to begin their march to the Palace of Westminster. The authorities were ready for them. The royal family had been dispatched to the safety of the Isle of Wight, barricades had been erected around major public buildings, such as the British Museum, which it was thought the rioters might have used as a fortress, and the Bank of England, which they might have plundered, and the military, bolstered by the police, were brought in. The message would be made clear: mob rule would not be tolerated in the capital. At first, the Chartists moved willingly from their assembly points around London to meet on the common in the south of London, where they were rallied with a rousing speech by Feargus O'Connor. But when they prepared to march back across the Thames towards Westminster, they were met with resistance. Only a small contingent was allowed across the bridge to take the petition, which O'Connor claimed had over five million signatures, to Parliament – where it was again rejected. In addition to the rejection, the leadership was made to look foolish when an official statement was released, giving the number of signatories as less than two million, with many of those being duplications and ridiculous forgeries.

Whether this was the truth or establishment 'spin' intended to debase and humiliate the leadership, the membership was disheartened by the futility of their efforts. But the labouring classes – as opposed to the disaffected poorest at the bottom of the social heap – were soon to have their minds on other matters as the economy began to crank into the gear that would witness a period of unprecedented economic boom and vast imperial expansion. Ironically, brute martial force and the success of capitalism had 'saved' the country from revolution, never mind that there were still many who were being excluded from its success and that the boom couldn't last for ever. Some might see parallels with the 'I'm all right, Jack' politics of the 1980s . . .

In the meantime, a strong economy meant that there was increased power for skilled workers, and strikes and demands for better conditions of employment became more frequent. However, the less privileged casuals or the unemployed were no better off than before. There were mass bread riots around the country, such as those in Deptford in London, during the winter of 1866 – 7, as prices rose and the poor went hungry. Bakeries and relieving officers became the target of crowd violence, which was then put down with little consideration of the circumstances under which the poor were expected to try to survive.

In the West Country, when the bread rioters clashed with the armed militia and special constables who had been hurriedly sworn in to help combat the mob, fighting broke out and a curfew had to be imposed. But the hardcore of the crowd were having none of it and they smashed and looted in Exeter until the early hours. They defended their actions by citing the price of the bread, claiming that the bakers and flour millers would rather let the rats eat the corn than sell loaves at a price the people could afford.

But if Thomas Wright's view, expressed in his 1892 work *The Pinch of Poverty*, was anything to go by, there wasn't a lot of sympathy for the starving poor:

In specially hard times . . . by driving the less patient of the honest poor to desperation and affording the more ruffianly of the no-visible-means-of-support classes an excuse for violence, lead to bread riots. In such times as these the relieving office is always in danger of attack . . . Bread or blood is the war-cry of the rioters on these occasions; but there are generally those amongst them whose desire is for bread and blood, and rather more for blood than bread. It is one of the functions of the relieving officer to thwart the designs of idle and habitual charity-hunters when they attempt to prey upon the forms of charitable relief by law provided. For this he is held in hatred by them, and a bread riot, in which members of this class

are always leading performers, is looked upon as an excellent oppor-
tunity for executing vengeance.

Something much worse than bread riots was to take place in February 1886. A mass meeting of the unemployed was held in Trafalgar Square, where demands were made for jobs rather than for voting rights. After the meeting, some of the demonstrators, who had been fired up by the stirring speeches, continued their march, making their way towards Hyde Park. They surged down Pall Mall, attacking the surrounding symbols of the wealth and privilege that they themselves so obviously lacked. Clubs, carriages and the expensive shops around St James's were set upon, and then the enraged mob moved on to loot parts of Oxford Street. For the next few days there were gatherings of mobs on both sides of the river. The original incident had caused enough panic among the powers that be for it to become known as Black Monday, and for the poor to be seen as nothing more than a terrifying mob, a criminal threat to law, order and all decent people. This perhaps goes some way to explaining the appalling reaction of the authorities in the following year – 1887 – when, on 13 November, a violent and brutal confrontation resulted in terrible injuries being inflicted on demonstrators by the police and their military back-up.

It might have been Queen Victoria's Golden Jubilee, but, as usual, the poorest of her subjects had very little to celebrate. Trafalgar Square and St James's Park had become nothing more than open-air doss houses for the unemployed, and the square itself had become a focus for campaigners demonstrating on their behalf, as well as for those protesting about the political situation both on the mainland and in Ireland. It was a pot ready to boil over. A major rally was planned for 13 November, with supporters first congregating at assembly points around the capital, from where they would march to Trafalgar Square. This was in spite of the fact that the police commissioner, Sir Charles Warren, had – eventually – succeeded in persuading the Home Secretary to impose a ban on meetings being held there. He had fought for this as a result of his fear of mob violence, which had become so acute that he had been regularly guarding the square every weekend, deploying up to 2,000 officers at a time.

Some of the marchers made it to the rally, but others were brutally cut off by mounted police and troops, with terrible injuries being inflicted on the thwarted demonstrators. Those who did get through, because they were approaching from different directions, were unaware of the police and military presence. When they arrived at their destination they found themselves surrounded and effectively cut off, trapped in Trafalgar Square. They were unable to escape as the police, the cavalry and the Grenadier Guards weighed into them, with massive contingents of special constables, who had volunteered out of fear of what the mob was capable of, making sure they were kept hemmed in.

Annie Besant, as a member of the Social Democratic Federation, was among those who took part in the demonstration that became known as Bloody Sunday for good reason.

As we saw earlier, Annie Besant and W. T. Stead were linked by their interest in Theosophy and the occult, but they also both wrote about issues that other writers shied away from. Always an activist, concerned particularly with the rights and conditions of women, in 1877 Besant had reprinted, with the radical Charles Brad-laugh, Charles Knowlton's *The Fruits of Philosophy*, a pamphlet about birth control. They realized that being able to control the size of their families was vital for the poor if they were ever to improve their lot, but such behaviour would not be tolerated by the Victorian authorities. Besant and Bradlaugh's efforts were rewarded with each of them being given a six-month prison sentence. This was overturned on a technical appeal, but just the possibility of imprisonment would have been enough to put off less determined individuals from their campaigning ways. Not so Annie Besant. Also like Stead, she went on to write about white slavery, but in her case she was referring to the plight of the match girls who worked at the Bryant and May factory in Bromley-by-Bow rather than the abduction of girls for the sex trade. Her actions would result in 1888 witnessing momentous events other than the shocking murders that took place in Whitechapel.

Annie Besant became involved with the match girls after

attending a meeting of the Fabian Society at which the working practices at the factory were exposed. She decided to see for herself what was going on there and waited at the factory gates to interview members of the young female workforce.

She recorded her findings on 23 June 1888, in her newspaper *The Link*:

. . . The hour for commencing work is 6.30 in summer and 8 in winter; work concludes at 6 p.m. Half-an-hour is allowed for breakfast and an hour for dinner. This long day of work is performed by young girls, who have to stand the whole of the time. A typical case is that of a girl of 16, a piece-worker; she earns 4s. a week, and lives with a sister, employed by the same firm who 'earns good money as much as 8s. or 9s. per week'. Out of the earnings 2s. is paid for the rent of one room; the child lives on only bread-and-butter and tea, alike for breakfast and dinner, but related with dancing eyes that once a month she went to a meal where 'you get coffee, and bread and butter, and jam, and marmalade, and lots of it'; now and then she goes to the Paragon [the music hall] . . . and that appeared to be the solitary bit of colour in her life. The splendid salary of 4s. is subject to deductions in the shape of fines; if the feet are dirty, or the ground under the bench is left untidy, a fine of 3d. is inflicted; for putting 'burnts' – matches that have caught fire during the work – on the bench is. has been forfeited . . . If a girl leaves four or five matches on her bench when she goes for a fresh 'frame' she is fined 3d., and in some departments a fine of 3d. is inflicted for talking. If a girl is late she is shut out for 'half the

day', that is for the morning six hours, and 5d. is deducted out of her day's 8d. One girl was fined is. for letting the web twist round a machine in the endeavour to save her fingers from being cut, and was sharply told to take care of the machine, 'never mind your fingers' . . . The wage covers the duty of submitting to an occasional blow from a foreman; one, who appears to be a gentleman of variable temper, 'clouts' them 'when he is mad'.

One department of the work consists in taking matches out of a frame and putting them into boxes; about three frames can be done in an hour, and 1 ½ d. is paid for each frame emptied; only one frame is given out at a time, and the girls have to run downstairs and upstairs each time to fetch the frame, thus increasing their fatigue. One of the delights of the frame work is the accidental firing of the matches: when this happens the worker loses the work, and if the frame is injured she is fined or 'sacked'. 5s. a week had been earned at this by one girl 1 talked to.

The 'fillers' get ¾ d a gross for filling boxes; at 'boxing,' i.e. wrapping papers round the boxes, they can earn from 4s. 6d. to 5s. a week. A very rapid 'filler' has been known to earn once 'as much as 9s.' in a week, and 6s. a week 'sometimes'. The making of boxes is not done in the factory; for these 2 ¼ d. a gross is paid to people who work in their own homes, and 'find your own paste'.

It wasn't just the manufacturing conditions that were so appalling; as Besant discovered, the workers had other grievances. One of these was an event that had happened a few years earlier, but was still resented by them. Bryant and Mays employees had been given the 'privilege of contributing' a shilling a week from their wages in order that a statue of Gladstone might be erected by his great fan Theodore Bryant. They had then been 'granted' a half-day's holiday – against their wishes – on the day of its unveiling. Of course, they had had to forfeit the half-day's pay, which was disastrous for the poorest among them. It summed up for the workforce the way they were thought of by their employers.

All this was bad enough, but there was a far more worrying aspect to working in the match factory. The employees were expected to work and eat whatever food they could afford to bring with them in the phosphorus-contaminated atmosphere of the factory. This put them at a very high risk of developing 'phossy jaw', a cancer that rotted the face – both skin and bone – and led to a horrible death. Phosphorus had been banned elsewhere, but the British government decided that to do so would restrict trade.

Following the publication of the *Link* article, three girls were sacked by the management for 'telling lies' and this resulted in a delegation of 200 workers marching to Annie Besant's office off Fleet Street to ask for her help. In her practical and determined way, Besant organized a strike, inviting management to sue her rather than taking out their anger on the sacked workers. She also arranged a carefully monitored strike fund to keep the workers in food and rent.

Not everyone was sympathetic to the strikers. The *Penny*

Illustrated Paper, for example, didn't approve of their actions at all:

> *The ostensible cause of the strike was the dismissal of a girl for disobedience of a managerial order; but, in reality, it is with the view of enforcing higher wages. Dating from the last Church Congress, when a gentleman of Socialist views read a paper in which he pointed out the high interest on capital and the alleged starvation wages to labour paid by Messrs Bryant and May, there has been simmering discontent among the girls working in the spacious and well-ventilated factory in Fairfield-road, a dissatisfaction which has been constantly fanned by addresses from members of the Social Democratic Federation and a body called the Fabian Society.*

The article failed to mention that as production increased an additional floor had been added to the top of the building, effectively stopping the little ventilation that had once been available to the workers.

Anyway, Besant worked hard at publicizing the strikers' cause among the great and the good. It took just three weeks for the company to agree to the majority of the match girls' demands, and their action was to be celebrated as one of the landmark successes of combined labour. With Besant's help, the workers had formed the Union of Women Match Workers, and they acquired premises paid for with the residue of the strike fund. By October of 1888, they were almost 700 strong - the original membership having been swollen by seasonal workers returning from the annual hop-picking harvest in Kent. By the end of the year, they had reorganized in a way that allowed men to become members, and so the Matchmakers' Union was born, an example of the success of collective action for the fledgling TUC, which had been formed twenty years earlier. Following the match workers' successful industrial action, the years between 1888 and the ending of the first World War would see union membership growing at its fastest rate ever. Queen Victoria's subjects were quickly realizing that they didn't have to stand alone any longer.

Another landmark in collective action was the 1889 gas workers' strike, as a result of which demands for the first ever eight-hour working day were accepted by management. It also saw the emergence of the union leader Will Thorne. Thorne, Tom Mann and the charismatic John Burns were to work alongside Ben Tillett, fronting the struggle for the 'docker's tanner' – in other words, to pay casual dock workers sixpence an hour and to give them enough hours to make up a reasonably paid working day.

Sufficient confidence had been generated by the spark of the new unionism for the discontented dock casuals to feel able to ask more of their employers. The seasonal, unpredictable nature of their work had traditionally had them being 'called on' solely when it suited the bosses – that is, when there was work to be done – and with only the fortunate members of the desperate crowd being selected. Ben Tillett described the cattle-marketlike atmosphere as the men stampeded their fellow casuals as they fought to be picked from the throng and to be granted a few hours' paid work. Despite their willingness – and their desperation – to be given work, there were no regular hours, and they and their families found themselves in a constant struggle to survive.

Nominally, the strike came about when employers cut the bonuses that were paid to casuals for working as quickly as possible, thus benefiting the dock and the ship owners. Matters were further complicated by a cyclical dip in trade, which meant the casuals were competing for fewer jobs. But these problems were superficial and there were other, deeper-rooted grievances that needed to be addressed.

Under Tillett's guidance the casual workers in the West India Dock downed tools. It didn't matter that they had no strike fund, because they were soon being supported by the skilled workers of the Stevedores' Union, without whose expertise the docks would fold. The dockers, with the backing and encouragement of their leaders, put out a call to members of other unions to support them, as well as asking the public to show their generosity.

The plea worked and the unions brought the docks and many other industries throughout London to a halt. According to the *Evening News* of 26 August 1889: 'The great machine by which five millions of people are fed and clothed will come to a dead stop, and what is to be the end of it? The proverbial small spark has kindled a great fire, which threatens to envelop the whole metropolis.' There were daily marches to Tower Hill, where rousing speeches were made to keep up the morale of the strikers. These meetings must have been impressive. When I interviewed a man in the early 1980s, he could still remember the excitement of the crowd as he was carried as a small boy through the cheering men, high on his docker father's shoulders. Collections were held at these rallies, and supporters from as far away as Australia sent large contributions, creating a strike fund which enabled the men to continue. The Australian donations in particular arrived at a crucial moment, when the strikers were coming close to being broken.

The restraint of the strikers was much admired, even in the press, and the *East London Advertiser* for 24 August 1889 compared the dockers who wanted nothing more than fairly paid work to the French, whose strikers, the journalist claimed, just demanded bread.

As the strike dragged on, the ship owners began to turn against what they saw as the recalcitrant dock companies, while the establishment fretted at the thought that a general strike was about to be called – a threat that struck at the very heart of Victoria's extraordinary empire. Meetings were called and after just five weeks almost all of the dockers' demands were met. The excluded had demanded, and won, inclusion, by showing, in the words of John Burns, 'its capacity to organize'.

There were many other episodes of industrial action during Victoria's reign as labour became more confident, but other events occurred that didn't have quite such a satisfactory outcome. Achieving a decent wage for a fair day's work by mass organization in the form of structured unions was eventually seen by the majority as a laudable aim – although this was to change in the twentieth century – but there were other groups of people operating at the time that found themselves gaining far less popular support. These were the groups that were associated with violent dissent, carrying out acts that would now be called terrorism – acts that were engineered by people coming from outside the mainland to wreak havoc and mayhem, spreading distrust and fear among us – an all too familiar tactic today.

In Queen Victoria's reign the main such group were the Fenians: the nineteenth-century incarnation of Irish nationalism. On the afternoon of 13 December 1867, a keg of gunpowder was ignited by the wall of the Clerkenwell House of Detention, in an attempt to free two prominent Fenian prisoners, Richard O'Sullivan Burke and Joseph Casey. The attempt was unsuccessful, and instead of breaking through the wall, the force of the explosion destroyed a nearby terrace of houses – obviously not so robustly constructed as the gaol. Twelve people lost their lives and 126 were injured in the blast. A few weeks later, an Irishman, Michael Barrett, was arrested in Glasgow and charged with causing the explosion and subsequent deaths and injuries. He was found guilty and condemned to death. On 26 May 1868, on a scaffold outside Newgate Prison, he became the last person to be hanged in public.

Barrett's execution didn't deter his compatriots and the

use of explosives continued as part of a concerted campaign that was carried out between 1883 and 1885. This included the first examples of terrorists targeting the London underground. On one day in October 1883 the line near Charing Cross was dynamited, followed by an explosion close to Praed Street Station. There were no deaths but many injuries. In the following January, an explosion was prevented when a device was found in a tunnel near Euston, but the authorities weren't so fortunate in February, when a bomb exploded in a cloakroom at Victoria. They did rather better when they discovered unexploded devices at Charing Cross, Ludgate Hill and Paddington stations. Intelligence also prevented a potential bomber boarding a train near Liverpool with packages of explosives. The success wasn't repeated in January 1885, when a device exploded on an underground train at Gower Street.

But it was an incident that took place in 1884 that thoroughly embarrassed the Metropolitan Police, despite the fact that no deaths ensued. An anonymous letter had been sent to Scotland Yard in 1883, stating that not only would Superintendent Williamson be 'blown . . . off his stool' but all public buildings in London would be dynamited on the same night – 30 May 1884. On the chosen night, just before 9 p.m., a huge explosion ripped through Scotland Yard, damaging not only the CID and the Special Irish Branch HQ, but totally demolishing Superintendent Williamson's office. As the building was empty at the time, deaths were averted, but people in a nearby pub and a passing cabman were injured by flying glass. True to the threats in the letter, further bombs went off: one in the basement of the Carlton Club and another outside the home of Sir Watkin Wynne, a prominent establishment figure. A further device didn't explode, but if it had the humiliation would potentially have been even greater than that caused by the colossal hole left in Scotland Yard earlier that night. The bomb had been placed at the base of Nelson's Column in Trafalgar Square, in a position that meant, had the dynamite detonated, the column would have come tumbling down. The Met's reputation was to be further damaged the following year.

John Gilbert Cunningham, from County Cork, was, like a lot of Irishmen in London during Queen Victoria's reign, living in lodgings in Whitechapel. The difference between Cunningham and the majority of his countrymen – those who had come to live on the mainland to seek work, trying to escape from poverty – was that he was a Fenian activist taking part in the continuing campaign of bombings. On 24 January 1885 he was discovered lighting the fuse of a bomb at the White Tower, in the middle of the Tower of London – then very much a working barracks. He was captured when buglers sounded the alarm and the gates were closed. Cunningham, along with Harry Burton, his accomplice, was arrested. When his Great Prescott Street lodgings were searched, detonators were found. Both Cunningham and Burton were arrested and subsequently found guilty. Cunningham was also found guilty of another offence – one which has horrible parallels with contemporary terrorism: two years previously, in 1883, he had planted bombs on the London underground. Fortunately, nobody died in those nineteenth-century events, which meant that the sentences given were penal servitude with hard labour rather than execution.

It might seem astonishing that the Fenians were planting bombs in the underground as early as 1883, and two years later within the confines of the Tower, but, also in 1885, they actually managed to detonate two explosive devices inside the Palace of Westminster itself. As with previous campaigns, much of the financing of the Fenian Brotherhood came from the Irish American population in the United States, donations being drummed up by many of the leaders, who were living there in exile, while depending on 'foot soldiers' such as Cunningham to plant the devices.

On the same day as the attack on the Tower, 24 January 1885, the Palace of Westminster was open to the public, as was then usual on a Saturday, and a Mr Green, his wife and her sister from Cork took the opportunity to pay a visit. While walking down the flight of stone stairs from Westminster Hall, the party of tourists found a bag, which they reported to the constable on duty. As the bag began to emit smoke, the officer knew that they were being confronted with what was then described as an 'infernal machine'. The subsequent commotion – Mr Green and the constable were both yelling 'Dynamite!' at the tops of their voices – alerted another officer, who came to help, but as the bag became increasingly hot the first constable tried to throw it away from them and it exploded. Mr Green and his companions were, of course, very shocked and suffered some injuries – both women had part of their clothing ripped off by the force of the blast – but the constables were much more seriously hurt as they were blown into the crater caused by the bomb. Other officers hurrying to their rescue were confronted with the two victims, one unconscious and one totally disorientated, both completely blackened by the blast. Meanwhile, as all this was going on, another device exploded, this time in the House of Commons, causing far more extensive damage to the fabric of the building, but luckily no one was injured.

Even the supposedly beloved person of the Queen was not safe from criticism, or even from physical attack. In the first year of her reign her belief that her lady-in-waiting Lady Flora Hastings was pregnant by Sir John Conroy – a man whom Victoria had thought 'too close' to her own mother before her death – saw the Queen putting Lady Flora through the indignities of a virginity test, which showed her to be still 'intact'. When it became known that the lady-in-waiting died soon after from the liver tumour that had made her abdomen swell, Victoria was booed at the races by a public increasingly displeased by regal behaviour and what was perceived as the royals' money-grubbing ways. Crowds mocked the Queen's fondness for her prime minister, Lord Melbourne, and when she appeared some people called out that she was about to become Mrs Melbourne, gloating over the rumour that she was to marry the much older man. She went on, of course, to marry Prince Albert, a man who was criticized across the board, from the radical to the popular press and in mocking music-hall-type songs, for being nothing more than a German gold-digger. Later in life, when Victoria declined to take part in public duties following the death of her husband, questions were asked about why the Queen should continue to receive such generous allowances from the civil list. There was even a widely circulated, anonymous pamphlet entitled *What Does She Do With It?* that examined the Queens finances and showed that she had no need for support from the public purse. The monarch had inherited handsomely from several sources and, anyway, she wasn't even doing anything in return for the funds she was taking. The Queen drove her detractors into an even greater frenzy when she asked for money for a dowry for her daughter's marriage settlement.

When, in 1871, Victoria finally obliged the country by making herself available for the State Opening of Parliament her actions were condemned by the critics, who claimed she was only doing it because her public funding was about to be debated. Making an occasional appearance wasn't enough to satisfy her humbler subjects either, and in May of 1887 she was booed during a visit to the East End. But these vocal and written criticisms were nothing compared to the assassination attempts made on Victoria between 1840 and 1882. Opinions differ as to whether there were seven or eight attempts, but the following agrees with the general and official view that there were seven.

Attempt number one occurred on 10 June 1840, when the young Queen was pregnant. She was in a carriage with Albert when seventeen-year-old Edward Oxford fired two shots at her. There was all sorts of inflammatory reporting that Oxford was an agent of various dissident groups and societies, and, in what was probably something of a compromise decision, he was declared insane – and so not guilty – but was detained in an asylum at Her Majesty's pleasure.

Two years later, in May 1842, 22-year-old John Francis took a pistol shot at the Queen as she was being driven along Constitution Hill, the same place where Oxford had made his futile attempt. Francis was found guilty of high treason and sentenced to death, but at the firm suggestion of the Queen the punishment was reduced to transportation for life. It is a matter of debate as to whether this 'weakness' on Victoria's part led to the next attempt on her life, because the day after the commuting of the sentence became public, John Bean made his bid. He too failed, when a young man standing close by was brave enough to grab him. Some people immediately assumed that he had only made the attempt because Francis had 'got away with it'. But as Bean's weapon was merely loaded with powder, paper and bits of old clay pipe, and as, on Prince Albert's insistence, it was revealed that Bean had intended to make his attack several days before John Francis's changed sentence was announced anyway, these assumptions were refuted soundly.

The next attack came in May 1849, when an Irishman named William Hamilton received seven years' transportation after shooting a powder-loaded pistol at the royal carriage. Then in May of the next year an ex-soldier pleasingly called Robert Pate struck the queen across the head with a cane as she was leaving the house of the Duke of Cambridge. He received the same sentence as Hamilton.

The Queen was to have a rest from would-be assassins for the next few years, and it was not until February 1872 that Arthur O'Connor took his shot at Victoria as she was driven into Buckingham Palace. In one hand he held the pistol – which was unloaded and not in very good working order – and in the other a petition calling for the release of Fenian prisoners. O'Connor received a flogging and a year's imprisonment.

The final attempt came in 1882, when Roderick Maclean fired a pistol – this time loaded – at the Queen on Windsor Station. The jury found Maclean not guilty due to reasons of insanity. The Queen was not pleased with the verdict as it had been based on an outdated law concerned with treason and she felt it was not giving the right message to her subjects, especially as this time the attack might well have proved fatal.

Yet the public are fickle, and at the time of the Golden and then the Diamond jubilees there were great outpourings of loyal affection in response to the general hullabaloo of a very successful propaganda drive. Although the adoration was still by no means universal, there were enough members of the public ready to stand and cheer for the press to report on the fervour of her subjects. In a genuine publicity coup, the Queen, using the power of the new technology and the craze for cartes-de-visite, decided to have a series of them made portraying the royal family Cartes-de-visite were not, as they sound, visiting cards, but black and white postcard-style photographs, which were collected and stuck into albums – the Victorian equivalent of the celebrity magazines bought by people today who try to get an insight into the lives of the rich and famous. The royal cards were bought in their millions by her possibly affectionate, maybe just curious, subjects.

Collecting of another kind – that of statistics and sociological information – was another major preoccupation for Victorians, particularly those concerned with crime and criminal behaviour.

9

POLICE, POLICING AND CRIMINAL TYPES

The police force has perhaps reached the most contempt-ible condition to which it is likely to fall, and it is doubtless disgraced by a number of men who exercise their functions so basely that they have brought not only ridicule but hatred upon the body they represent. The majority of police-con-stables, however, are capable of better things; and there are still in the force men who, under a different regime, would do credit to the once popular ideas of detective sagacity and discriminative protection. The worst of it is that the very men who are totally unfit to hold the office of public protectors are those who become furious under the implied sentiment with which they are regarded. There are many officers in the force who seem to go out on duty with the feeling that, as they are probably regarded with dislike, they will take every opportunity of 'showing about it' by an exercise of the very considerable powers with which they are invested; and, as those with whom they chiefly have to do are people whose social influence is small, and whose good characters may not be very readily or easily substantiated by acceptable witnesses, there is ample opportunity for the most outrageous assertion of authority.

Penny Illustrated Paper, 6 December 1873

*

Up until the creation of the Metropolitan Police force in 1829, parishes had depended for their protection from criminals on the watchmen and parish constables, alongside the informal 'persuasiveness' of rough justice being meted out privately within the communities themselves. But the work of the watchmen and local constables was not always appreciated and distressing stories, such as the one that follows, were to be found in the press as their conduct and corruptibility came to be questioned more frequently This piece about the Bethnal Green watch was published in 1825, four years before the Metropolitan Police Force was established. It comes from the Tower Hamlets Local History Archive, where the source is not given:

The brutality of night-constables and watchmen in this metropolis, has been long attested by the daily records . . . These men are now an intolerable nuisance, in place of being a protection; they are a pest. For all good purposes they are utterly inefficient – for all evil ones they are prompt and capable. The street tyranny exercised by many of these ruffians is revolting. In several districts they exact a regular tribute, in money and drink, from the wretched females [the prostitutes] who shiver round them. A sop to the Cerberus stops his growl; a refusal consigns the shrinking victim to a watch-house; there she may pine the night in cold and darkness, to be dragged the next morning to a police-office, represented as incorrigible, by the brute she could not bribe, and on his swearing be sent for months to the tread-mill. Hitherto this despotism abstained at least from life; it paused on this side murder. But an inquest has been [made] public this last week, which has roused universal horror, and the evidence before the jury, we unhesitatingly assert, called for a verdict of felonious homicide against the watchmen who were accessories to the death of the unfortunate Anne Ashley . . . The wretched woman was found dripping with wet, and insensible from liquor, at two, on an inclement morning, at the east end of the town; she was taken to the watch-house of Bethnal-green, and given in charge to Simkins, the night-constable. In place of being suffered to remain before the fire, round which this brute and his myrmidons [hired brutes or rough, low servants] were circled, the unfortunate woman, who was drenched with rain and frozen by the night air, was dragged away and flung in to the dark hole of the watch-house. This was a narrow dungeon six feet square, with a gravel floor, streaming with damp, and reeking with human ordure. In this sink of pestilence, she was immured for four hours, and then was turned out by the mandate of the same savage, and thrown senseless and expiring, against the walls of the watch-house. In that state she died. And can there be a doubt that she was murdered — barbarously and deliberately murdered? We assert nothing in which we are not borne out by the highest legal authority. The Coroner, on the first day's investigation, took on him to state that there was no criminality imputable to the night-constable, and watchmen, and that the only conclusion the jury could come to was, that the conduct of these parties was very negligent. Say you so Mr Unwin [the coroner]? Is such an opinion warranted by either fact or law? That, however, we shall soon see. To what, we ask, did this unfortunate owe her death? Was it not to the horrible treatment she experienced in the watch-house? The surgeon examined before the Jury swore her death was occasioned by wet and cold, combined with intoxication; he added, that the dungeon into which she was thrown was a most unfit place to confine any one, especially one in the condition of the deceased.

Mr Coroner Unwin thought the conduct of this night-constable did not amount to manslaughter; and the Jury, under his direction, returned a verdict – 'that the unhappy woman died from the effects of cold and intoxication' – expressing a determination at the same time to prosecute the constable and watchmen for a misdemeanour, at the Sessions. We say they ought to be tried for murder. To make this atrocious homicide a misdemeanour is outraging justice. The constable was the gaoler of this watch-house, he confined his prisoner forcibly in a filthy, damp, and pestilential dungeon, from the effects of which she died, and the killing in law is murder. She was flung into this vault in a morning in November – saturated with wet, and chilled by cold. Could any constitution stand such an ordeal? Is there a man [who] on reflection can believe, that if this wretched woman, had been placed before the watch-house fire, and suffered to remain until she became sensible, and heat and animation were restored, that her life could have been in any danger? No, to think otherwise is ridiculous. The constable and watchmen caused her death, and they should stand at the bar of justice for their lives. We care not what the rank or character of the victim may have been – whether she was a peeress, or a prostitute is to us the same. The constable and watchmen, on the evidence before the Coroner, were her murderers; and they are homicides in law. If they are guiltless, let the judges of the land and a jury say so; but to blink the thing by calling it a misdemeanour, is one of the grossest jests on justice we have ever heard. The jury in this case acted well, admirably well; they sifted the foul deed to the bottom, but they were misled in their verdict by the language of the Coroner, who, in our apprehension, mis-stated both fact and law.

Despite the authors lack of confidence in what had gone before, there was a widely held perception that the newly organized police force had been brought in for the protection of the rich and their property at the expense of the freedom of those who were not so fortunate, and they too were not universally well supported, particularly within the poorer neighbourhoods.

In his *Sketches in London* of 1838, James Grant wrote about this distrust of the 'Met':

The new police were for some time very unpopular. There was a natural tendency in the minds of the people to look with suspicion on a body with very enlarged powers, and which had been constituted in a manner different from any previous constabulary force, which had been known in this country. These suspicions were converted into positive apprehensions by the clamorous opposition got up to the new police by one or two journals circulating largely among the lower orders of the community. Every movement they made was narrowly watched; and every action they performed was made the subject of severe criticism – often of downright misrepresentation. The result was, that the public prejudice, especially as regarded the working classes in the metropolis, became so strong against the new constabulary force, that the impression began to gain ground that the experiment – for it was admitted by Sir Robert Peel and others to be in some respects nothing more than an experiment – would not succeed, but that the body must be broken up, and a recurrence to something like the old system take place.

But the intentions behind setting up the force appear honourable enough, if Sir Richard Mayne, the first joint commissioner, is to be believed:

The primary object of an efficient police is the prevention of crime: the next that of detection and punishment of offenders if crime is committed. To these ends all the efforts of police must be directed. The protection of life and property, the preservation of public tranquillity, and the absence of crime, will alone prove whether those efforts have been successful and whether the objects for which the police were appointed have been attained.

His was perhaps an over-optimistic, rose-tinted view, if he believed that this could actually happen.

Friedrich Engels's opinion was rather more jaundiced,

and in his book *The Condition of the Working Class in England* of 1845 he noted the aversion to legal authority, although maybe he was overstating the case a little: 'The contempt for the existing social order is most conspicuous in its extreme form – that of offences against the law . . . with the extension of the proletariat, crime has increased in England, and the British nation has become the most criminal in the world.'

At least he was right about the contempt in which the law was held in some quarters. The following is from a court report in the *East London Observer* nearly forty years after the force had been introduced. The aims Commissioner Mayne had aspired to obviously hadn't yet been attained: 'Brutal assaults, particularly on the police, have been very frequent; and one ruffian – Jeremiah Donovan – was committed for trial for wounding a police constable . . . by striking him on the head with a piece of hard wood.' It was reported in addition that another 'ruffian of the same calibre', Patrick Maypowder, was charged with assaulting a policeman, this time near St Katharine's Dock. He had four convictions for similar attacks on constables. The police were frequently seen as merely interfering.

This incident, reported in the *Penny Illustrated Paper*, also occurred in the 1860s, showing that certain places were becoming almost 'no-go' areas for the force, as the rookeries had been in earlier part of the Queen's reign, and the Old Nicol, in Bethnal Green, would become by the 1890s:

At the Clerkenwell Police Court . . . Patrick Horsley and John Darling were placed at the bar before Mr D'Eyncourt, charged with rescuing a prisoner from the custody of police constables John Boolyer and William Miller, and assaulting them in the execution of their duty, at Golden-lane . . . The prisoners it was stated, are part of a desperate gang of thieves that infest Golden-lane. On the previous Thursday the above-named officers apprehended a prisoner [there] on charge of a felony, and when on the way to the police-station they were beset by a gang of rough fellows and thieves, and their prisoner rescued from them. They [the police] again captured the man, but had not proceeded far before both constables were knocked down and kicked in a very brutal manner. Both the officers stated that they were very much hurt about the head and body, and they now felt great pain.

But from their very earliest days, Metropolitan Police officers had been the objects of violence. In 1829 PC Joseph Grantham was killed while carrying out his duties in the tough area of Somerstown, in Euston. In 1831 police fought a running battle with a rioting crowd that was attacking the Duke of Wellington's home, Apsley House, in London. Then, in 1833, there was another death of a policeman PC Robert Cully, in the riots that broke out on 16 May in Coldbath Fields, Holborn, at a meeting where workers were gathering to try and organize for better pay. As a contemporary broadsheet described the incident, there was a 'Dreadful Riot in London':

A Full, True, and Particular Account of that Great Public Meeting which took place in Coldbath-fields, London, on Monday last, for the purpose of forming a NATIONAL CONVENTION, giving an account of the Speeches delivered on the occasion – Together with an account of the desperate attack made on the meeting by a body of 3000 Policemen, under the direction of Lord Melbourne, and Colonel Rowan and Mr Mayne, – with the names of the killed and wounded, and the number taken prisoners.

This time there were publicly expressed accusations that the police had acted with unnecessary vigour against the crowd. These complaints didn't come only from those involved in the event, and in the court case against the person accused of the police officers murder, the jury agreed. The stated intentions of the police, that they were there to keep the streets free from theft and violent crimes against the person, had rung hollow, just as when the force was deployed to put down political demonstrations such as those of the Chartists, and did so in such a brutal way. There was a major outcry at the time, much the same as when people objected to the police being deployed during the News International disputes in 1986.

And it wasn't only members of the public who were criticizing the conduct of the Metropolitan Police. In 1863 drunkenness was such an ongoing problem within the ranks that in that one year alone over 200 officers had to be sacked because of their inappropriate behaviour. It actually wasn't unusual for the public, as well as fellow criminals, to 'protect' offenders from the law. The back door of a pub would be left unlocked so that if police officers entered the premises to arrest someone, the guilty party could shoot out through the back and escape to freedom. Similarly in the rookeries, a door would be opened to let someone run in and along the passageway and then disappear among the rabbit warrens of the interconnecting hovels – if the police were brave enough to enter the maze of slum dwellings in the first place.

Calls of 'Boot him!' were regularly reported as being shouted by gangs of the so-called 'lower orders' as they rallied together in a combined effort against the police

– the very gangs who, ironically, before the arrival of the officers, had been fighting with one another. Put simply, the police continued to be equated with repression rather than protection; they were seen as being there to represent the allegedly respectable haves in society against the have-nots. But there were also accusations that they 'took care' of wealthier criminals, as they weren't averse to taking bribes from those bad lots who were more than happy to forfeit some of their illegal profits in exchange for an officer turning a blind eye to their activities.

When the police caught a wrongdoer, what happened to him or her depended on the seriousness of the offence – and some offences were taken astonishingly seriously, especially before the removal of what had become known as the Bloody Code. This comprised the series of punishments that had begun to be introduced following the social and political upheavals of the seventeenth century, again with the main and evident intention being to protect the property of the minority haves from the majority have-nots. By 1750 crimes for which someone could be executed had risen to 160, and by 1815 the number had increased again, this time to an amazing 288.

These 'crimes' for which an individual could be hanged – in a public execution – included being in the company of gypsies for a month, cutting down a young tree and, perhaps most shockingly, children between the ages of seven and fourteen could be executed if they showed 'strong evidence of malice'.

But it has to be said that by the beginning of Victoria's reign, the code had been weakened considerably, and the ultimate price no longer had to be paid for those accused of such trivial matters as stealing a letter or a sheep, or pilfering goods worth five shillings or less. Serious crimes, however, could still find the culprits being executed, transported for life, issued with heavy fines that they had no hope of paying or being subjected to a brutal whipping. When shorter sentences were given – from a few days' to a couple of years' detention – they were served in Houses of Correction, otherwise known as the Bridewells, after the eponymous building in London. With containment rather than punishment being the point of these institutions, they also served as places to hold individuals who were awaiting trial. Regardless of the fact that the crimes for which these 'lighter' sentences were being served were considered to be at the petty end of the criminal scale, the inmates were still subjected to hard labour. Originally, this wasn't used just as a form of punishment – although that was an important consideration – but also as a way of making money for the unpaid overseer of the convicts, who had actually had to buy his position as keeper of the gaol, so profitable could the position be. He would then sell the fruits of the inmates' labours in the marketplace and take the profits as his wage. He would also charge for any special privileges, though obviously only from those prisoners who could afford them. Those who did have the means could live in some style, having food and drink delivered to them and servants waiting on them. Because it was so open to corruption, this arrangement had to be changed, as did the organization of the prison system as a whole.

Following the abolition of most of the Bloody Code, imprisonment itself became the punishment for the majority of crimes. Before the 1840s, long prison sentences had not been usual, except in the case of debtors, and criminals were either transported to the colonies or were hanged. Yet despite the – to us – appalling conditions in Victorian prisons – the pointless and demeaning hard labour, the almost starvation rations and the use of the cat-o'-nine-tails – or the cruelty of transportation to the colonies for children as young as six years old, in terms of punishment, criminals in this period were a lot better off than their predecessors had been. Despite the changes, conditions still varied throughout the country and prisons were still being run autonomously by their keepers in old, insanitary buildings, with no differentiation being made as to who was held in them. This resulted in a dangerous and pitiless mix of every type of 'criminal', from the mentally ill adult to young children who had been accused of trivial offences.

A report on the conditions in prisons showed that they ranged from the brutal to the ridiculously lenient, and it had reformers demanding changes and improvements to the system. These weren't purely philanthropic concerns, however, but the result of serious anxieties arising from the spread of urbanization. Traditional communities were breaking down, or even disappearing, and a fear of the mob and the criminal classes grew as the masses descended on what seemed to be the ever-expanding towns and cities. Something had to be done. A supervised, national prison system had to be introduced. As a result of these calls, new buildings went up and different regimes were tried out.

These regimes included the silent and the separate systems, which were similar to those being employed in America. These methods were introduced partly in response to the idea that crime was a disease that could be passed on to others like a contagion. This meant that communication between inmates had to be prevented at all costs, and also that the convicted persons would have plenty of time and opportunity in which to contemplate their crimes in total silence or solitude, and so to repent and mend their ways. For the separate system, prison buildings were designed to ensure that there could be no possible opportunity for social intercourse between the inmates. Even when attending religious services, sinister hood-like caps hid the inmates' features; these were also worn during exercise, when each convict held on to a rope knotted at specified intervals that denoted the distance to be kept between them, so prohibiting any form of contact. Punishment in the separate system had to be something worse than solitary confinement – although the authorities were careful to call the system *separate* confinement – and it was. The convict would be kept in a special cell where no light could penetrate; so, they were kept in total darkness, on rations of dry bread and water, for anything between a few days to three weeks. It should not have been too difficult to predict that suicide rates would shoot up under these arrangements. The authorities' response was to bring in extra exercise periods, but the rates still remained higher than under other regimes.

In addition to what must have been this quite soul-destroying solitude, there was the meaningless, repetitive work that had to be carried out by the prisoners. In the separate system this would be done in isolation in the same space in which they lived and slept – their cells; and in the silent system, work was done under strict supervision to ensure that no one spoke. But as Henry Mayhew and John Binny noted in 1862, in their *Criminal Prisons and Scenes of London Life*, the drive to communicate is so strong that the prisoners made every effort to have some form of contact with one another as they did their pointless tasks, despite the threat of further punishment:

But if it be difficult to prevent prisoners from audibly talking with each other, it is next to impossible, even by the most extensive surveillance, to check the interchange of significant signs among them. 'Although there is a turnkey stationed in each tread-wheel yard,' says the Second Report of Inspectors of Prisons for the Home District, 'and two monitors, or wards-men, selected from the prisoners, stand constantly by, the men on the wheel can, and do, speak to each other. They ask one another how long they are sentenced for, and when they are going out; and answers are given by laying two or three fingers on the wheel to signify so many months, or by pointing to some of the many inscriptions carved on the tread-wheel as to the terms of imprisonment suffered by former prisoners, or else they turn their hands to express unlockings or days.'

Remarkably, the treadmill would not be taken out of commission until 1902, a year after Victoria's death.

Shot drill was another meaningless job that prisoners were expected to carry out. It involved passing each one of a pile of cannon balls from one end of a line of inmates to the other – all supposedly in total silence – where they were stacked up in another pile before the whole lot were passed back all over again, and again. There was no point in the task other than that it was back-breaking and demeaning, just like the treadmill and the crank.

The crank was favoured in the separate system, as it could be fitted in individual cells. It had a counter and a heavy handle that had to be turned a specified number of times for hours on end, the resistance being increased by the warden, who could adjust the mechanism at his will, thus making it even harder to turn.

A less physically demanding but still painful task was picking oakum, an activity, like the treadmill, also favoured by advocates of the workhouse system, who were determined, as we have seen, to deter malingerers. This involved the inmates unravelling old salt-and tar-ingrained ropes, rendering them back to individual strands, which were then reused for caulking ships. Physically it was very hard on the hands, but, as with the other meaningless 'work', there was the psychological torment suffered, brought about by the repetitive mundanity of the task.

In his 1874 book *The Wilds of London*, James Greenwood recorded the experience of a young man sentenced to three years' penal servitude who was given oakum to pick as part of his daily labour:

At half-past six [in the] morning the prison bell rang for getting up, and as soon as I was dressed a warder opened a little trap in the door, and put through into my cell a small brush and a dustpan, at the same time telling me to make my place tidy, and when I had swept up, and folded away my hammock on the shelf; he brought me a piece of cloth and told me to polish the floor, which . . . was of asphalt, and would take a sort of shine if rubbed long enough. When that job was done, my day's work was brought to me, consisting of a pound and a quarter of oakum. Along with the oakum was an iron hook, with a strap to it, and this was to fasten to the knee to help tear the tarred rope, which is as tough almost as catgut. A pound and a quarter does not seem much, and it doesn't look much – a piece as thick as a man's wrist and as long as his hand would weigh a pound I should say – but a pound and a quarter of it to a man whose fingers are as soft as a woman's, and who hasn't the least idea how to go about it, is a tremendous day's work. I knew that for the first four or five days I was at work on it from morning till night, with my nails broken and my fingers bleeding, and even then it was not done so well as it should have been – at least, so the warder said . . .

There was another pressing reason why more prisons needed to be built: transportation was no longer seen as a suitable means of punishing criminals – especially within the colonies themselves. Influential people were beginning to agree with Henry Mayhew's view that the practice wasn't so much populating the colonies as polluting them. By the 1850s, transportation had become limited to those prisoners whose sentences were for fourteen years or more – which may be a little strange, considering the avowed reasons for not wanting the practice to continue – but at last, in 1867, it was abolished altogether.

Running parallel to this, an opinion was emerging that not only were the silent and separate systems inhumane, but they weren't even a deterrent – as could be seen from the crime statistics. These showed that crime rates had gone up and reoffenders were continuing to account for over 25 per cent of the prison population. Whether the figures had risen because of a genuine increase in crime or, as was suggested by some at the time, because a more efficient police force was catching more criminals, they remained a problem. Before the County and Borough Police Act of 1856, criminal statistics had been unhelpful in that they referred to committals as opposed to incidents of crimes or to criminals apprehended. An example of the distortions this could cause was given in the parliamentary inquiry cited by Rob Sindall in his 1990 book, *Street Violence in the Nineteenth Century*. Fourteen people with 'a constant habit of making and uttering false coin' had each and every coin counted as a separate offence, meaning that, according to the statistical system then being used, they had committed 20,000 offences between them. Another example of the misleading nature of statistical collation in the period occurred when the age of majority was raised from fourteen to sixteen, making it appear – in the short term at least – as if the number of juvenile offenders had suddenly surged upwards. The 1856 Act went some way to dealing with the anomalies, but statistics will only ever be as useful as the manner in which they are collected and interpreted, and how the parameters are defined. Sindall, for instance, makes the important point that infanticide hadn't been classed as murder but as 'concealment of birth', meaning that the coroners' records and the crime statistics didn't tally regarding unlawful deaths of babies and young children. And with new categories being added to the statistical records in 1857, it appears as if crime had indeed rocketed.

Definitions, categorization and interpretations continue

to present us with problems, affecting not only statistics but also our feelings towards particular crimes. But we should certainly not be smug in our judgements of people's reactions to the reporting of these events: even with today's sophisticated collection techniques, there are real doubts as to the validity of crime statistics, though the experience of crime for its victims remains all too real. A newspaper report on the Audit Commission in London's *Evening Standard* from December 2004, for instance, quoted a district auditor as saying: 'The crime figures could be right, they could be wrong. We just don't know.'

This statement, however, has to be considered alongside real events affecting actual people. At the very time that the Audit Commission report was being published, an 82-year-old woman was attacked and robbed by a gang of schoolgirls, who beat her and left her sprawled on the ground with a broken arm. She refused to press charges for fear of reprisals. If she had been told that youth crime was on the decline, and that it was fear of crime that was the real problem, it wouldn't have made much difference either to her very real fears or to the injuries she had suffered.

And, for instance, while attitudes are changing, seeing abuse within the home as 'domestic violence', rather than the physical assault or murder that it is, has allowed such crimes to be widely dismissed as 'just a domestic'. Even now some judges are calling for convicted, but sufficiently 'contrite', domestic abusers to be let off from facing custodial sentences.

But back in the good old days, it wasn't only the use of solitary confinement, corporal punishment, the poor food and hard labour that was attracting the attention of the reformers, it was also the escalating costs of the system, and theorists were coming up with all sorts of ideas about how best to deal with what were now being described as the 'criminal classes'.

Schooling of youngsters was considered one possible way to reduce the prison population. As this editorial in a December 1863 edition of the *East London Advertiser* suggested:

> *Our costly system of penal servitude is found practically a lamentable failure, and the conviction gains ground daily among all save bigots and enthusiasts whom facts, however palpable, will not unhorse from their favourite hobby, that by an immediate return to transportation alone will public security and public tranquillity be effectively restored . . . we must not shut our eyes to the fact that Beelzebub's recruits are mainly drawn from among those who, with deliberate intent, are sedulously kept beyond the sphere of the school room, during the very years when mental culture is most readily instilled . . . Indeed it is perfectly notorious that a great majority of our juvenile felons receive their first instruction from the prison school-master, and such 'old sparrows' are proverbially difficult to tame.*

The ragged schools, which provided education for the very poorest, could have come into their own here, providing potential juvenile felons' with instruction in the three Rs, hygiene and scripture, thus at least possibly equipping them with the means to find legal ways of making a living as an alternative to the life of crime – whether of the petty or more serious kind – for which most of them would otherwise be heading. Not all the schools had the same purpose or aims, but they all offered this free basic education to the very poorest of children, who were also fed and clothed to a standard that would otherwise have been out of their reach, in a warm, clean school, and some could even attend classes where they learned practical working skills to help them find legitimate jobs.

But despite all the inducements, not every youngster was willing to accept the opportunities being offered, however well meaning the school organizers might have been. In an annual report from one of the schools that was published in the year before the *East London Advertiser* editorial, the children are described as being uneducatable in the ways and manners of decent people. It seemed that even the very youngest of them were already well versed in foul language, chewing and smoking tobacco, and other things that are left to the imagination – being described merely as 'vice'. There were more hopeful views from those working within the Ragged School Union as to the impact that they could have on young people's lives, but this was by no means the official opinion.

In an 1861 Report into Education in England, one of the commissioners, Patrick Cumin, quoted by Claire Seymour in her 1995 book *Ragged Schools, Ragged Children,* stated that juvenile crime had declined in Bristol, but in Plymouth, a city where there existed a more 'fully developed' system of ragged schools, juvenile crime had 'largely increased'. But the school unions would not be deterred and, even after the 1870 Education Act, which provided access to schooling for all children between five and thirteen years of age, they continued to do what they could for the very poorest young people. The last ragged school in London was not closed until 1910.

Not everyone was as concerned as the school unions were with prevention, reform or even rehabilitation, and there were those who just wanted to find more efficient ways of catching the 'habitual criminals' so they could put them away, out of the reach of decent people. One such means involved the use of the rapidly improving new technology of photography. This was to produce the striking mug shots which, from the middle of the century, were being seen as a way to enhance police records and aid investigation. The photographs were filed away with a note of the criminal's identity, age, height and any distinguishing features; in addition, there were details of the crimes that had been committed, the resulting court cases and subsequent sentencing. By the 1870s prison governors were being ordered to take photographs of all their inmates which they were then obliged to pass on to the commissioners of police. This practice was extended and copies of the photographs had to be deposited with registers of the criminals' convictions in offices in London, Edinburgh and Dublin.

As can be seen by this increasingly centralized organization, number crunching and in the work of social investigators such as Henry Mayhew and Charles Booth, there was a confidence that order and categories could be imposed and identified by the application of new technology and scientific, empirical observation. The time was right for the work of Cesare Lombroso to come into its own.

This Italian physician and professor of psychiatry, known as the founder of criminology, believed that crime was the result of biological destiny rather than either the product of environmental factors or a matter of simple choice. In his 1876 book *The Criminal Man*, he explained his theory that the criminal was nothing more than a throwback, a creature like Neanderthal man, who was born and not made. This beast could be identified by the atavistic 'stigmata' displayed in his anatomical formation. These were numerous, and some, such as an imbalance in the hemispheres of the brain, having too many or too few ribs, inverted sexual organs or peculiarities of the palate, 'such as those found in some reptiles', could only be identified by intimate or post-mortem examination. But Lombroso listed plenty of other signs that would be obvious after even a cursory glance at someone's physiognomy. These ranged from having ears of unusual size, or standing out 'as do those of the chimpanzee', to having a turned-up, flattened or twisted nose if the person was a thief, or a beak-like nose in the case of a murderer.

Lombroso went on to argue that as the behaviour of

these criminal types was biologically determined there was no point in trying to reform them or to save them from themselves. Instead he became an advocate of sterilizing these odd-looking individuals so that they couldn't reproduce more of their kind. Presumably, crime would eventually disappear, along with their seed.

This social Darwinism fitted perfectly with the mentality of the advocates of the colonial free-for-all that was raging throughout the nineteenth century, pillaging its way around the world. It allowed for the colonialists to be seen as obviously superior and so there by right. It also supported the retention of privilege by the rich and powerful at home, as the theory 'proved' that they had succeeded by nothing less than biological destiny.

If the 1930s and 1940s hadn't witnessed what a eugenics project actually entailed, Lombroso's ideas might well still be in favour today.

Do we really want to return to those good old days?

CONCLUSION

Whilst we have been building our churches and solacing ourselves with our religion and dreaming that the millennium was coming, the poor have been growing poorer, the wretched more miserable, and the immoral more corrupt; the gulf has been daily widening which separates the lowest classes of the community from our churches and chapels, and from all decency and civilization. It is easy to bring an array of facts which seem to point to the opposite conclusion – to speak of the noble army of men and women who penetrate the vilest haunts, carrying with them the blessings of the gospel; of the encouraging reports published by Missions, Reformatories, Refuges, Temperance Societies; of Theatre Services, Midnight Meetings and Special Missions. But what does it all amount to? We are simply living in a fool's paradise if we suppose that all these agencies combined are doing a thousandth part of what needs to be done, a hundredth part of what could be done by the Church of Christ. We must face the facts; and these compel the conviction that this terrible flood of sin and misery is gaining upon us. It is rising every day. This statement is made as the result of a long, patient and sober inquiry, undertaken for the purpose of discovering the actual state of the case and the remedial action most likely to be effective.

Andrew Mearns, *The Bitter Cry of Outcast London*, 1883

*

Rather than being the good old days, we have seen that during her time on the throne, Queen Victoria was witness to a most unruly reign, and that this country could be a bloody and an awful place in which to live – unless you were fortunate enough to be a member of the privileged classes and, even better, if you were male into the bargain.

At the beginning of the period, things were very different for those who weren't as lucky as their social 'superiors'. Women and children were working in the coal mines, tiny boys were being sent up chimneys, the age of consent was just twelve years old, incest was almost a given in the worst of the overcrowded slums, excessive use of alcohol and the abuse of drugs caused terrible social problems, and casual violence was taken to be a feature of everyday life. By the end of the Queen's reign, some things had changed a great deal, such as the move from the countryside to the towns and cities, and the rapid progress in technology, as seen, for example, with the introduction of the first motor vehicles. The *Penny Illustrated Paper* called it 'The Talk of London':

The car will be put 'before the horse' with a vengeance shortly . . . it is left for the fin de siècle to make horseless carriages successful. The legislature [has] cleared the way. A Bill passed last Session removed the ban against motor cars in this present month of November [1896]. Sir Harry Lawson conclusively proved by his easy manipulation of a petroleum impelled carriage in the Lord Mayor's Show . . .

It might have been fine for the likes of Sir Harry, but progress hadn't touched everybody in the same way. In his 1903 book *The People of the Abyss*, Jack London recalled an incident when he was living in London in the year following Victoria's death. He was accompanying a carter and a carpenter along the Mile End Road as they made their way to Poplar Workhouse:

From the slimy sidewalk, they were picking up bits of orange peel, apple skin, and grape stems, and they were eating them. The pips of green gage plums they cracked between their teeth for the kernels inside. They picked up stray crumbs of bread the size of peas, apple cores so black and dirty one would not take them to be apple cores, and these things these two men took into their mouths, and chewed them, and swallowed them; and this, between six and seven o'clock in the evening of August 20, year of our Lord 1902, in the heart of the greatest, wealthiest, and most powerful empire the world has ever seen. These two men talked. They were not fools. They were merely old.

Yet we still bemoan the fact that things are not like they used to be and insist that everything was so much better back then. That golden age discourse has retained its power, with commentators looking back at how social problems would be solved if we went back to the values of the past, instead of seeing – and celebrating – the fact that our society is, on the whole, maturing, with a developing awareness that we should be tolerant of different views, an improved understanding of child welfare, better behaviour towards animals and a realization that assaulting and even killing your spouse is rather more than a 'domestic'. But the chorus continues to be heard that the world around us is deteriorating in every possible sense.

Bad behaviour, which then goes on to become criminal, was – and still is – seen as the fault of the 'other'. This pertains, regardless of whether the 'other' is defined as being from another class, another age or another ethnic group. Or it results from a lack of moral fibre, poor parenting, deficient education or doubtful genetic make-up. But instead of merely describing and inciting horrified reactions as to what is occurring, why are we not analysing the situation and striving to come up with some sort of strategy? Yes, we are horrified by crime and fearful of it in all its manifestations – from the trivial to the tragic – but what does that sort of reaction achieve? And what is the point of talking about ever-changing short-or medium-term solutions, or punishment and rehabilitation, when what would suit everyone is prevention?

Then the question becomes – what sort of prevention? Gates, bars, more police, stricter laws? These are all fine, but how about inculcating aspiration in young people and providing attractive alternatives to crime before we set up the barricades against our neighbours' children? I certainly know that I don't believe that the answer lies in a return to Victorian values.

*

As I sit here catching glimpses of a past that intrigues and sometimes dazzles, I am also shocked by it, because for every achievement enjoyed by Victoria's more advantaged subjects, I cannot help but acknowledge that her world would not have been very kind to me. The notion of entitlement to any kind of decent opportunities being extended to the likes of me, a female born in the East End, whether it be access to power, the vote, reasonable health care, anything more than a very rudimentary education and most of the other, what we now take to be basic human rights, in between.

When I was a schoolgirl we were moved out of London during the time of the slum clearances to a council estate in Dagenham. No matter that it wasn't a place where my mother ever felt settled – my parents eventually moved out to rural Essex – but the house was warm, clean and actually had a bathroom and a garden. How different from the conditions in which Victorian cockneys were expected to live, such as those described here in *The Bitter Cry of Outcast London* by Andrew Mearns:

Here are seven people living in one underground kitchen, and a little dead child lying in the same room. Elsewhere is a poor widow, her three children, and a child who had been dead thirteen days. Her husband, who was a cabman, had shortly before committed suicide. Here lives a widow and her six children, including one daughter of 29, another of 21, and a son of 27. Another apartment contains father, mother, and six children, two of whom are ill with scarlet fever. In another nine brothers and sisters, from 29 years of age downwards, live, eat and sleep together . . . Where there are beds they are simply heaps of dirty rags, shavings or straw, but for the most part these miserable beings find rest only upon the filthy boards. The tenant of this room is a widow, who herself occupies the only bed, and lets the floor to a married couple for 2s. 6d. per week. In many cases matters are made worse by the unhealthy occupations followed by those who dwell in these habitations. Here you are choked as you enter by the air laden with particles of the superfluous fur pulled from the skins of rabbits, rats, dogs and other animals in their preparation for the furrier. Here the smell of paste and of drying match-boxes, mingling with other sickly odours, overpowers you; or it may be the fragrance of stale fish or vegetables, not sold on the previous day, and kept in the room overnight. Even when it is possible to do so the people seldom open their windows, but if they did it is questionable whether much would be gained, for the external air is scarcely less heavily charged with poison than the atmosphere within.

And these were the 'fortunate' ones who didn't have to resort to the common lodging houses, tenement stairwells, railway arches, under a coster's barrow or, worst of all, the workhouse.

Things were rather different for the middling classes, as can be seen in this description of their lives by the American writer David V. Bartlett in his 1852 book *London by Day or Night*:

In the English heart there is a deep love of quiet, calm enjoyments, and home joys – this is the reason why the English home is so lovable . . . In England the holidays, even in London, have a rural tinge . . . Englishman gathers his children about him, and goes to spend the day at Epping Forest, Gravesend, or Kew Gardens. It would be no pleasure for him to wander over the fashionable walks of the city, but away from the crowd, in the bosom of his family, he indulges in the height of felicity.

Among the middle classes in England, or perhaps we should say the upper-middle, there is no degree of want, but rather profusion of all that can minister to the respectable appetites of mankind. The house, the grounds, the situation and prospect are nearly perfect. We have seen many English homes and never for once came away from one without an enthusiastic admiration of the sweet garden in which it pleasantly nestled. Painting ministers to the eye, and music to the ear.

In the morning at nine the father sits down cosily with his family to his dry toast and coffee, his morning newspaper and family letters, devouring them all together. The Times with fresh news from all quarters of the world lies open before him, and the 'resonant steam eagles' have been flying all night that he may read his letters with his morning meal. He then starts for his counting-house, or his office, and with a luncheon at mid-day satisfies his appetite until the dinner-hour – which is at four, five, or six, as circumstances may be – when he dines with his family around him. Tea is served at seven, a simple but generally a very joyous meal. Supper is ready at nine or ten, of which the children never partake. A true English home is intelligent, educated, and full of love. All that Painting, Sculpture and Poetry, can do to beautify it, is done, and Music lingers in it as naturally as sunshine in a dell.

As Andrew Mearns observed, the surroundings of the squalid homes of the poor hardly offered an encouragement to the slum dwellers to go out for a healthy constitutional and fill their lungs full of air. We worry, rightly, about our environment now, but the horse-and cattle-dung-slicked streets, coal-fired industry, heating and cooking, and the lack of basic sanitation must have made for an atrocious mix in Victorian times. These caused more problems than just dirtying the hemlines of ladies' skirts, thickening the peasouper fogs, known as London Particulars because of their distinctive, sulphurous yellow colour, and the smelly bodies and bad teeth.

Apart from the stench and general unpleasantness there were, more seriously, the diseases and the epidemics that cut through the slums, with rarely little more than the most basic of medicines for the masses, plus guesswork and quackery, to combat them. Henry Mayhew, in his usual statistically well-informed way, lists the numbers of destitute poor who sought help for the following conditions in just one year at one refuge. Together with cases of pregnancy, these health problems included:

Catarrh and influenza; Incipient fever; Rheumatism; Diarrhoea; Cholera; Bronchitis; Abscesses; Ulcers; Affections of the head; Ague; Excessive debility from starvation; Inflammation of the Lungs; Asthma; Epilepsy; Atrophy; Dropsy; Incised wounds; Diseased Joints; Erysipelas; Rupture; Cramps and pains in bowels; Spitting of blood; Lumbago; Rheumatic ophthalmia; Strumous disease; Sprains; Fractures.

By the end of the Victorian era life expectancy at birth was still just forty-two years. On the whole, I would rather take my chances with antibiotics, a free health service and reliable contraception.

But even if you were blessed enough to be healthy and were willing to look for employment, there was again the problem of the lack of opportunities. It was very unlikely that anything more than poorly paid, casual work would have been offered to those from the unskilled labouring classes, as those who had not had the benefit of a decent education would have been. And, as Mayhew informed the shocked better-off classes, the women would sometimes feel they had no alternative but to turn to prostitution.

So, coming from my background, I would have had numerous children whom I would have had trouble feeding, clothing and keeping warm and dry. And I would have been denied the chance of using my mind for anything other than trying to come up with ways of making ends meet – which would more than likely have meant selling myself, if I was still capable of such a thing.

William Acton, following his own investigations into prostitution, wanted to help the women return to respectable society, which he thought they would do once they were too old to work, rather than when they found some preferable way to make money. But he didn't ask what the women would do if there wasn't any alternative employment available to them:

One mistaken notion, the fallacy of which I have already exposed, lies at the root of the penitentiary system. The old idea, once a harlot always a harlot, possesses the public mind. Proceeding from this premiss, people argue that every woman taken from the streets through the agency of penitentiaries, is a woman snatched from an otherwise interminable life of sin, whereas I have shown that the prostitute class is constantly changing and shifting, that in the natural course of events, and by the mere efflux of time the women composing it become reabsorbed into the great mass of our population – and, in fact, those whom the penitentiaries receive are those who are weary of, or unfit for their work, and in search of some other mode of life. The reasonable course to adopt is to assist the natural course of things; to bear in mind that sooner or later the life of prostitution will be quitted, and that the duty of society is to accelerate so far as possible the change, and in the meantime to bring such influences to bear on abandoned women as shall enable them to pass through their guilty years with as little loss of self-respect and health as possible; how to render the prostitute less depraved in mind and body to cause her return as soon as possible to a decent mode of living, to teach her by degrees, and as occasion offers, self-restraint and self-denial, to build her up, in short – since join society again she will in any event – into a being fit to rejoin it, is the problem to be solved. Will not this be more easily and satisfactorily accomplished by subjecting all alike to supervision and bringing them into daily contact with healthy thought and virtuous life, than by consigning to wearisome and listless seclusion a few poor creatures snatched at haphazard from the streets?

He may have been sympathetic to the women's lot, but his work didn't make much of an impression on the numbers of them working in the sex trade. When money was needed, the women 'worked'.

The changes in the age of consent which resulted from the crusades of the likes of Stead and Butler to protect young girls from sexual exploitation is something that we surely must now applaud, but this is one area in which I believe we are being hypocritical. The commercially moti-vated sexualization of ever-younger children surrounds us in styles of clothing, including T-shirts with explicitly sexual slogans and chain-store underwear for even pre-teens that wouldn't look out of place in an 'adult' shop.

But even here I suppose it could be argued that those children are benefiting from the choices we are so lucky to be given in our twenty-first-century society, and that it is those very choices that make life so much sweeter than that experienced by people of the same classes back in the nineteenth century Opportunities have certainly come with those choices, and we have been moving gradually towards a meritocracy, and a long way away from the world where people like me would have lived a life that, in the words of Thomas Hobbes would have been: 'poor, nasty, brutish, and short'.

Finally, as people live longer and, in so many ways, easier lives, we should not be looking back to a fictitious golden age of the past, but forward to a silver age of the future, in which grey-haired silver foxes are able to enjoy what has come to be known as their adultescence, a time of life that would never have been achieved in the past – well, certainly not by the likes of me.

A GLOSSARY OF SOME SLANG TERMS, FOLLOWED BY VICTORIAN MONEY

Some of these words, many of which have their origins in Victorian times or earlier, are still in use to this day, if rather less frequently than in the past. But, from my childhood, I can remember much of the language explained here being in common usage in the East End, especially among men of my father's generation – a man who was born immediately after the First World War and so, of course, to Victorian parents. Many examples of nineteenth-century slang, particularly words used by criminals, have their origins in a far earlier period and have then filtered through to the present day – just as the words below have come to be understood by me through the usage I learned from my elders. What follows is a selection of those that are still just holding on, or maybe have just slipped over the edge of obscurity.

Area: pronounced 'airy': the entrance to the lower ground floor of a dwelling, usually reached via stone steps

Aris: backside: convoluted piece of back slang – aris = Aristotle; Aristotle = bottle; bottle = bottle and glass; bottle and glass = arse; probably most familiar today when used in 'losing your bottle' or 'bottling out'

Baggage: tart, prostitute

Barney: fight

Bastille: workhouse

Beak: magistrate

Beat: watchman's, and later constable's, walk

bit faker: *see* coiner

blab: to tell secrets

black diamonds: coal

Black Maria: vehicle used to take prisoners to gaol

Blag: to steal or snatch

block house: prison

blow-out: really good, satisfying meal

bob: shilling

bog trotters: pejorative term for the Irish

bolt: to run away

bounce: swagger, as in 'he's got some old bounce'

brass sauce or cheek, as in brass neck; later, prostitute, probably from the cheap brass 'wedding rings' worn for the sake of respectability

bread basket: stomach

break a drum: burgle a house

bride: prostitute

britch: pocket, as in 'I'll stick it in my back britch'

broads: playing cards; also the three-card trick or other dodgy card game

bubble: to swindle or cheat; later, to inform

bug hunting robbing or conning drunkards

bully: pimp, sometimes pretend husband to prostitute

bunts: clandestinely raked off profit from 'dodgy'

cadger: beggar

cane: jemmy, used for breaking and entering; ironic name, associating it with the cane carried by gentlemen

case house: brothel

caser: five shillings

cat: prostitute, particularly one who is drunk and fit for a fight child

chav or chavvie: child: (from Romany); now used as disrespectful term for a stereotypical white, working-class person who dresses in knock-off designer clothes and is seen as uneducated and liable to antisocial and immoral behaviour

cheye-ike: barracking

chiv: sometimes pronounced 'shiv': knife, noun and verb

claret: blood, particularly that spilled in a fight

cleaned out: having lost all your money, usually by gambling

coiner: maker of counterfeit coins

collar: to snatch; later, also to arrest

conk: nose or sneezer

coopered: no longer any use, worn out, as in today's knackered or over, e.g. 'bit-faking is a coopered racket' coppers: loose change, non-silver coins

cosh: sometimes called a 'life preserver': a loaded stick or iron bar, often cited as being used by criminals in garrotting cases when used to subdue the victim

crack a case: to burgle a house

crib: to steal; also room in lodgings

Crown and Anchor: gambling game

Cut: to avoid or shun someone

Daddler: farthing

Deaner: shilling

Derby Kelly: belly

Ding: to discard something

Dip: pickpocket

Doss house: common lodging house, kip house, spike

Dragsman: thief who robbed cabs or carriages by climbing up from behind and pinching the luggage off the roof

Dropsy: money; sometimes used specifically for a 'bung', i.e. bribe

Drum: someone's home, whether in a house or lodgings

Duds: clothes

Flash: showy

Flash house: pub frequented by criminals

Flimp: to steal something from someone, not in a skilled pickpocket's style but rather by snatching

Game: brave

Gelt:(from Yiddish) money

Glimms: lights, eyes

Gonnoff: (from Yiddish) thief

Grass: informant

Green: ignorant, uneducated

Greenhorn: countryman, yokel

Groin: ring, as in jewellery (claimed by some to be of later origin, but used in my family much earlier and so a good example of the 'slippery' nature of slang)

Gull: to cheat or con

Hoister: first used for a pickpocket; later, and more commonly, for a shoplifter

Hoof it: to walk

Ivories: the teeth

Jacks: five pounds, from Jacks alive – five

Jacksy: backside

Jug: prison

Kecks: also kicks: trousers

Kettle: watch, usually the pocket variety

Kidsman: trainer and organizer of child thieves

Kincin lay: stealing from children

Kip house: common lodging house, doss house, spike

Ky-bosh: to turn the tables on someone; later, to spoil, as in 'to put the ky-bosh on someone or something'

Lamp: the eye: also to thump, as in 'he's lamped him!'

Lugs: ears

Mooey: face

Mug: also mug punter: not criminals, but their target

Muller: to murder someone – from the first railway murderer, Franz Mulle

Mump: scrounge

Mumper: beggar, cadger

Napper: the head

Nicks: also nix: nothing

Nip: cheat, noun and verb

Peter: safe, occasionally used for prison cell

Peterman: safe breaker

Phizog: the face

Pimp: also ponce: man living off immoral earnings

Pitch and Toss: game, also known as Pieman, involving flipping two halfpennies or pennies, which with the palming of double-headed coins could be very profitable as the banker won every time the coins came up both showing the same face

Pogue: purse or wallet; later, also money, as in having 'a bit of pogue' in your pocket large bag or sack

Pony: money, fifty pounds

Pop: to pawn

Pot herbs: mix of root vegetables sold by costers, used to stretch stew of sheep's head, scrag end or another cheap cut of meat, much as supermarkets sell 'stew packs' today

Racket: criminal activity, as in 'What racket are you in?'

Ready: also readies: money

Ring: to illicitly exchange one item for another

Roll: stealing from a drunk, as in 'rolling a lush'

Rozzers: police

Schneid: also snide: counterfeit, as in 'that's a snide', to describe, maybe, a phoney Victorian diamond ring that was being passed off as genuine, or, today, a supposedly designer handbag

Schtook: also stook, stuke, stock: the usually white scarf/kerchief worn round the neck, as part of the costers' and cockneys' 'uniform'; in its earliest use a handkerchief

Scran: food

Screw: to go out robbing, as in 'out on the screw' or 'to go screwing'; originally from 'screw' meaning key, rather than our contemporary association with sex, but certainly a link with our slang for prison officer

Sky: pocket – from 'sky rocket', as in 'I'll stick it in me sky'

Slop shop: sweat shop

Spieler: unlicensed gambling club, often in a room above a shop in and around Whitechapel or Aldgate; drinking or luxury wasn't the point – big money changing hands was

Spike:common lodging house, originally the workhouse

Sprazzy: sixpence

Starring the glaze: breaking a windowpane to enable a burglary

Swag: stolen goods; later, inexpensive, flashy, usually shoddy articles for resale by hawkers, market traders or cheap shops

Swag shop: wholesale supplier of swag (I would go to them with my father when I was a little girl and I thought I was entering Wonderland or Aladdin's cave)

Tanner: sixpence

Tanner hop: dance for which sixpence is the admission

Tec: detective; word used in one of the letters supposedly sent by Jack the Ripper and still used by my father to denote someone in the CID as opposed to Old Bill, meaning the police in general

Tile: hat

Titfer: tit for tat – hat

Togs: clothes

Tombstones: teeth

Topped: hanged; later, also murdered hanged, married; later, to have been conned

Twig: to observe; later to latch on to something

Twirls: keys, as in a burglar having a 'set of twirls'

Van dragging: stealing from the backs of vans and carts

Wedge: silver plate; later, money

Coins in circulation during the period

Farthing: a quarter of an old penny (¼ d)

Halfpenny: penny pronounced 'ha'penny' (½ d)

Penny: a twelfth of a shilling (1d, 240 to the pound)

Two-penny piece: pronounced 'tuppence', a sixth of a shilling (2d)

Groat: a four-penny piece, a third of a shilling (4d)

Sixpence: shilling half a shilling (6d)

Shilling: twelves pennies (1s or 1/-, twenty to the pound)

half a crown crown: two shillings and sixpence (2/6 or 2s 6d)

crown: five shillings (5s or 5/-)

half-sovereign: ten shillings (10s or 10/-)
sovereign: twenty shillings or a pound (£1)

By the Victorian period the guinea was no longer a coin but was equivalent to twenty-one shillings (£1 1s). Expressed in multiples, it was used by professionals for their fees, posh shops and for the sale of thoroughbred horses.

A BRIEF CHRONOLOGY

1837: death of William IV; Victoria becomes Queen

1837 – 44: major economic downturn – the 'Hungry Forties'

1838: Chartists present their first petition to Parliament

1839: Custody of Infants Act: allows for women of 'unblem-ished character' to see their children following divorce or separation

Metropolitan Police Act: introduces £2 fine for prostitution
   Chartist demonstrations

1840: Victoria marries Prince Albert
   penny postage begins in Britain
   construction of Pentonville Prison begins
   Select Commitee on Health of Towns reports on slum conditions
   Chartist demonstrations

1841: UK population is 18.5 million
   first edition of *Punch*

1842: publication of Edwin Chadwick's sanitary report, which exposes the hygiene problems for the poor being caused by industrialization Factory Act: limits the working day of women and children between thirteen and eighteen years of age in the textile industry to twelve hours, while children under thirteen have their hours reduced from nine to six and a half per day; but the legal age for employing the children is reduced from nine to eight Mines Act: prohibits women and children under ten years of age from working underground

Chartist demonstrations and the Plug Riots plain-clothes detectives instituted in the capital

1843: Nelsons Column placed in Trafalgar Square Theatre Act: theatres permitted to sell food and drink; this would lead to the spread of the music halls

1844: appearance of Colonel Tom Thumb in London at the Egyptian Hall

1845: Victoria Park in east London opens

1846–9: Irish potato famine

1847: Clerkenwell House of Detention opens

Factory Act: reduces the working day of women and children in the textile industry to ten hours.

Poor Law Commission abolished after the scandalous conditions in Andover workhouse are discovered, to be replaced by the more answerable Poor Law Board

James Simpson introduces medical anaesthesia

1848: publication of Marx's *Communist Manifesto* revolutions sweep across continental Europe

Chartists are held by police on Kennington Common

W. H. Smith opens first station bookstall first music hall opens

1848–9: over 60,000 die of cholera in England, Scotland and Wales

1850: Factory Act: changes working hours for women and children to 6 a.m. – 6 p.m., with a hour's break, Monday to Friday, and 6 a.m. – 2 p.m. on Saturday, essentially increasing the working day overall

1853–4: over 25,000 die in cholera outbreak, 10,000 in London alone

1854–6: Crimean War

1855: removal of newspaper stamp duty sees massive expansion of the press

1857: Indian Mutiny

Matrimonial Causes Act: establishes secular divorce – a man can divorce on grounds of his wife's adultery, but a woman cannot be granted divorce because of her husband's adultery, having to prove extreme cruelty, desertion, incest or some other cause

1859: publication of Darwin's *The Origin of Species*

1863: estimates of numbers of prostitutes in London range from 5,500 to 80,000 first underground line in London opens

1864: First Contagious Diseases Act

1865: the Ladies of Langham Place organize a petition calling for a Women's Suffrage Bill

1866: over 17,000 die in cholera outbreak, 6,000 in London alone

Second Contagious Diseases Act

1867: Joseph Lister introduces use of antiseptics

1868: Gladstone becomes prime minister

1869: Debtors' prisons abolished

Third Contagious Diseases Act, extending its powers

1870: Married Women's Property Act: permits women to keep £200 of their own earnings'; also, they can inherit personal effects and small amounts of money, but anything else, regardless of whether they owned it before marriage, belongs to their husband

1872: Public Health Act: set up to appoint medical officers of health and sanitary authorities

1874: Disraeli becomes prime minister

Factory Act: raises minimum working age to nine years

1875: Public Health Act: gives sanitary authorities the regulation of water, drainage and sanitation

1876: invention of the telephone

1878: first electric street lights introduced in London

1880: Gladstone becomes prime minister

1881: population of London rises to 3.3 million

Smoke Abatement Committee set up

1884: Married Women's Property Act: makes a woman a person in her own right rather than a chattel of her husband

Special Branch set up to deal with crimes affecting the security of the state

1885: Royal Commission on the Housing of the Working Classes publicizes the poor housing conditions in London and other cities National Vigilance Society established as self-appointed moral guardians trafficking for the sex trade

1886: Guardianship of Infants Act: allows for a woman to become sole guardian of her children if her husband dies

Black Monday riots in London

1887: Bloody Sunday in Trafalgar Square

1888: Bryant and May match girls' strike Whitechapel Murders

1889: London dock strike

1890: global flu epidemics

1893: Labour Party is formed

1898: the Curies discover radium

1899–1902: Boer War in South Africa

1900: publication of Planck's quantum theory

1901: Factory Act: raises the minimum working age to twelve years

Death of Queen Victoria

BIBLIOGRAPHY

Selected sources and suggestions for further reading.

Acton, William, *Prostitution: considered in its moral, social and sanitary aspects in London and other large cities and garrison towns. With proposals for the control and prevention of its attendant evils*, John Churchill and Sons, 1870 edn

Anonymous, *Sinks of London Laid Open: a Pocket Companion for the Uninitiated, to which is added a Modern Flash Dictionary containing all the Cant Words, Slang Terms and Flash Phrases now in Vogue, with a list of the sixty orders of Prime Coves*, J. Duncombe, 1848

Archer, Thomas, *The Terrible Sights of London and Labours of Love in the Midst Of Them*, S. Rivers & Co., 1870

Bartlett, David V., *London by Day or Night, or Men and Things in the Great Metropolis*, Hurst and Co., 1852

Beames, Thomas, *The Rookeries of London: Past, Present and Prospective*, T. Bosworth, 1850

Besant, Walter, *East London*, Chatto and Windus, 1901

Booth, Charles, *Life and Labour of the People in London*, Macmillan, 1892-1902

Chesney, Kellow, *The Victorian Underworld*, Victorian Book Club edition, 1971

Diamond, Michael, *Victorian Sensation*, Anthem Press, 2004

Fisher, Trevor, *Scandal: The Sexual Politics of Late Victorian Britain*, Alan Sutton Publishing Ltd, 1995

Fishman, William, *East End 1888*, Duckworth, 1988

Gamman, Lorraine, *Discourses on Women and Shoplifting*, unpublished PhD thesis, 1999

Grant, James, *Sketches in London*, W. S. Orr, 1838

Greenwood, James, *Low-Life Deeps: An account of the Strange Fish to be found there*, Chatto and Windus, 1881 edn

— *The Seven Curses of London*, Stanley Rivers and Co., 1869

Harrison, Brian A., *The Tower of London Prisoner Book: A Complete Chronology of Persons Known to Have Been Detained at Their Majesties' Pleasure 1100 – 1941*, Royal Armouries, 2004

Jackson, Louise A., *Child Sexual Abuse in Victorian England*, Routledge, 2000

Jones, Rev. Harry, *East and West London*, Smith, Elder and Co., 1875

Lamont, Peter, *The Rise of the Indian Rope Trick: How a Spectacular Hoax Became History*, Abacus, 2004

Manby Smith, Charles, *Curiosities of London Life*, William and Frederick Cash, 1833

Mayhew, Henry, *London Labour and the London Poor: a cyclopaedia of the conditions and earnings of those that will work, those that cannot work and those that will not work*, 4 vols., Dover unabridged reprint, 1968, of original 1861 – 2 edn

— *London Labour and the London Poor*, edited by Victor Neuburg, Penguin, 1985

Mearns, Andrew, *The Bitter Cry of Outcast London*, 1883, reprinted Leicester University Press, 1970

Morton, James, *East End Gangland and Gangland International Omnibus*, Time Warner, 2003

Pearsall, Ronald, *The Table-Rappers: the Victorians and the Occult*, Michael Joseph, 1972

Pearson, Geoffrey, *Hooligan: A History of Respectable Fears*, Macmillan, 1983

Rumbelow, Donald, *The Complete Jack the Ripper*, W. H. Allen, 1987

Samuel, Raphael, *East End Underworld*, Routledge, 1981

Sandhu, Sukhdev, *London Calling: How Black and Asian Writers Imagined a City*, HarperCollins, 2003

Sanger, 'Lord' George, *Seventy Years a Showman*, Dent and Son, 1926 edn

Seymour, Claire, *Ragged Schools, Ragged Children*, Ragged School Museum Trust, 1995

Sindall, Rob, *Street Violence in the Nineteenth Century*, Leicester University Press, 1990

Stedman Jones, Gareth, *Outcast London*, Clarendon Press, 1971

Sugden, Philip, *The Complete History of Jack the Ripper*, Robinson, 1994

Sweet, Matthew, *Inventing the Victorians*, Faber and Faber, 2002

Thomas, Donald, *The Victorian Underworld*, John Murray, 1998

Young, G. M. (ed.), *Early Victorian England*, OUP, 1934

There are many interesting websites associated with the period, but I would always caution against using material from the Internet, especially without making several checks with authoritative secondary sources, or, even better, primary sources where available. I would, however, recommend *uMms.victorianlondon.org*, which is a site containing many fascinating primary sources. Similarly some academic sites have full-text versions of Victorian books, pamphlets and investigations. Again, even with reputable academic sites, I would always suggest that their contents are checked against the original works, as the information given online is only as reliable as the person inputting the data from the primary material.

I am indebted to the ever-kind, patient and professional staff at the various institutions where I was able to consult national and local newspapers from the period, as well as more specialized periodicals, pamphlets and publications, reports and conclusions of investigations, as well as popular novels, broadsheets and contemporary photographs and artefacts. I found the main sources for these materials in the following places:

Barbican Library Bishopsgate Institute British Library
British Library newspaper collection at Colindale
Guildhall Library
London Library
Museum of London
Tower Hamlets Local History Archive

ENDEAVOUR INK

Endeavour Ink is an imprint of Endeavour Press.

If you enjoyed *The Good Old Days* check out
Endeavour Press's eBooks here:
www.endeavourpress.com

For weekly updates on our free and discounted eBooks sign up
to our newsletter:
www.endeavourpress.com

Follow us on Twitter:
@EndeavourPress